D1498966

ISBN: 9798676835224

First Edition

V.7-11.07.2020

The 3:15 Project is a long-overdue answer to prayer in a digital age. It's helping people move from 'scared to prepared' in sharing their faith. But not only that, it exponentially increases the exposure of their stories for Gospel results we could only dream about a decade ago.

Scott Smith
Georgia Baptist Mission Board

The 3:15 Project has the potential to launch a generation of bold, humble, and courageous Christians.

Chuck Bengochea
Former CEO of Honeybaked Ham and Family Christian

I'm a huge believer in helping leaders steward their time and resources. The 3:15 Project gives churches of any size an efficient and effective way to empower their people to share their story, outside the walls of the church, with professionalism and authenticity.

Bryan Miles
Co-Founder of BELAY

The 3:15 Project has tremendous power to unleash a fresh wind of evangelism within and beyond the United Methodist Church.

Larry Malone
Former President of the World Fellowship of Methodists

The 3:15 Project is very powerful. It's right at the heart of the Great Commission, sharing the Gospel, penetrating darkness, and growing believers.

Tommy Ferrell
Pastor, Briarlake Church

The 3:15 Project is filling a HUGE need in the Church and I urge you to take advantage of this opportunity.

Carmen Fowler LaBerge
President, Layman.org

The 3:15 Project gets Christians out of the pews and onto the battlefield.

Walt Wilson
Global Media Outreach

Very few churches in America have the equipment and personnel resources, as well as expertise, to do what The 3:15 Project can do. Regardless of your church's size, I encourage you to utilize this tremendous resource that The 3:15 Project offers.

Billy Phenix
Northpoint Ministries

Helping men who love Jesus have the opportunity to memorialize and share their story in such a wonderful way is one of the best ministry investments I've ever made.

Regi Campbell
Founder, Radical Mentoring

Sharing your story authentically, from the heart, is one of the best ways to evangelize and spark interest in another person to come to know Jesus...The 3:15 Project is the perfect answer.

Most Reverend Michael J. Byrnes
Auxiliary Bishop of Detroit

The 3:15 Project is primed to play an even bigger role in the time ahead as the Church seeks to carry out the call to actively engage in the new evangelization.

Father John Riccardo
Our Lady of Good Counsel

I'm a huge believer in the impact of The 3:15 Project. I have seen firsthand how it helps draw people closer to Jesus, and each other.

Fritz Weise
Pastor, Christ Our Shepherd Lutheran

I believe that God is moving in and through, The 3:15 Project and have witnessed how it helps people come into a deeper relationship with Jesus Christ.

Scott MacLellan
CEO, Touchpoint Services

I believe The 3:15 Project's willingness and ability to train young people to film and harvest stories within their local communities and churches would be a catalyst for an exponential movement of evangelism and discipleship within the local Church.

Dennis Nunn
Every Believer a Witness

STORIES OF HOPE

Vol 1.

DEDICATION

This book is dedicated to anyone and everyone who yearns to be loved and love others more deeply. May you be open-hearted and willing to receive the infinite love of Jesus Christ.

For this reason, I kneel before the Father, from whom every family in heaven and on earth derives its name. I pray that out of His glorious riches He may strengthen you with power through His Spirit in your inner being, so that Christ may dwell in your hearts through faith. I pray that you, being rooted and established in love, may have power, together with all the Lord's holy people, to grasp how wide and long and high and deep is the love of Christ, and to know this love that surpasses knowledge—that you may be filled to the measure of all the fullness of God. Now to Him who is able to do immeasurably more than all we ask or imagine, according to His power that is at work within us, to Him be glory in the church and in Christ Jesus throughout all generations, forever and ever! Amen.

Ephesians 3:14-21

ACKNOWLEDGMENTS

The stories within this book and the book itself would have never been possible without many people, more than we can possibly name or thank, selflessly giving their talents, time, treasure, wisdom, prayers, love, and of course their stories.

Brian Cork, Matt Stevens, Mark Montgomery, Rob Consoli, Chuck Bengochea, Sonny Newton, Jeremie Kubicek, Billy Mitchell, Larry Clayton, Bruce Paulk, David Montgomery, Daniel Roberts, Josh Sims, George Kinyanjui, Billy Phenix, Sean Seay, Andy Stanley, Jeff Henderson, Randy Walton, Susan Conley, Kevin Shaw, Len Sykes, Larry Green, Kevin Latty, Bob Lewis, Boyd Bailey, Burke Allen, Jay Hassell, Steve Taylor, Chad Jackson, Steve Kaloper, Bill Stark, Jason Montoya, Bryan and Shannon Miles, Joel Manby, Scott MacLellan, Stanton Lanier, Walt Wilson, Dan Hitzhausen, George Landolt, Rusty Gordon, Larry Malone, Regi Campbell, Chris Hornsby, Mark Butler, Travis Dommert, Josh Webb, T.J. Campbell, Andrew Schoppe, Stokes Mayfield, Kevin Harris, Mike Morris, Lyndon Carr, Maureen Dierkes, Bill Blane, John Posey, Diane Grant, Monique Maksym, Carmen LaBerge, Jim Rizer, Peter Ruppe, Mary Martin, Julie Hixson, Fr. Ben Kosnac, Ian Locke, Michael Jones, Bart Newman, Christopher Hunnicutt, Eric Smith, Jessica Lalley, Wayne Hilton, Greg Austin, Bob Carter, Payton and Andrea Mayes, Todd

Porter, Kevin and Katherine Malone, Marcus Graham, Chris Collinson, Ginger Jones, Charlie Paparelli, John Hanger, David and Jill Felts, Peter Bourke, Bill Platten, Brooks Lalley, Zach Hanger, Mike Bishop, Jay Thompson, Fr. John Riccardo, Steve Mitchell, Kris Yankee, Brett Davis, Michael Tablada, Brett Saunders, Charles Lumpkin, David Smallwood, Tommy Ferrell, Mark Granger, Brian Clark, Dan Miller, Mike Long, Bob Jolly, Delton de Armas, Michael O'Neil, Fritz Wiese, Brad Jubin, and many others for which we are extremely grateful.

A special thank you to Carla Armstrong, Marcus Raven, Kris Castro, Todd and Jenny Sorenson, Paula Wallace, and Ginny Priz for co-laboring on this book.

A very special thanks to my parents, my wife Kim, my boys Ian, Owen, and Aaron, and my teachers for always encouraging me, challenging me, and never giving up on me.

Most of all thank you to Jesus for so freely and lavishly loving us and giving us a reason for hope.

Todd Miechiels
3/15/2020

Contents

FORWARD

I've had the incredible honor of serving God as a pastor for 25+ years. I've been blessed to share God's word and encourage people to follow Jesus hundreds of times. When you get the opportunity to do this, you never know what the results will be. But I consistently pray God will help people take the truth of His word and apply it to their lives. Every time it happens it blows my mind. It fills me with joy.

When I spoke at Buckhead Church in 2010, I had no clue who Todd Miechiels was, or that he was in the room. I had no idea the story God was writing in his life. But as I've watched God at work in his life and the hundreds of stories that have exploded from that time I am overwhelmed. It brings me so much joy to see people taking courageous steps of obedience

God is so personal. He's writing a story in your life. He obviously led you to this book. I'm praying that as you read and watch these stories, He builds your faith and leads you toward greater obedience. I'm praying these stories will remind you of God's great power to change lives. I'm praying He will help you see His power in your life. May He give you eyes to see His amazing patience and kindness toward you. May He help you see His activity in your life today and a vision of His dreams for your future.

When you read the Bible, you see God is a God of stories. He's writing a grand and beautiful drama. Your life is a part of that story. May the stories in this book help you better understand the story God is writing in your life and help you know the power of sharing it.

Sean Seay
Pastor Athens Church

INTRODUCTION

The stories found within this book are precious. They were harvested from men and women all over the country. Seemingly every day ordinary people who were all interrupted with a simple but powerful question. *Would you be willing to share your story?* Not just share their story, but do it in such a way that the world could see it, where they couldn't take it back, *on video,* and let it be published to the internet. Some initially declined such a jarring proposition, others wanted to pray about it first. One woman without hesitation, simply and quite beautifully said *"How could I not?"* Everyone is this book, and hundreds more who weren't included in this first of what will hopefully be many volumes, made a conscious decision both in their head, and in their heart to lay down their fears, their pride, and their busyness and trust God.

These stories are just a small portion of what has become a significant and growing collection of testimonies, lovingly cultivated, and harvested by The 3:15 Project and our incredible ministry partners.

Each of these storytellers were led through a guided journey we call *Steps of Courage*. This journey is an intentional pathway which helps people know and share their story wholeheartedly. The stories that you are reading and can watch online, are the evidence, the result, and the fruit of each of these storytellers first making a decision to abide with Jesus, making themselves available to Him and our ministry team, and trusting the process while leaving the outcome to God.

Our prayer is that you won't simply read these stories, but you'll also listen to, and watch them. Look into the eyes of God's beloved sons and daughters. Listen to their heartfelt words of hope and encouragement, even as they themselves have endured pain and heartache, victory, and joy. May these stories speak and minister to your heart, drawing you ever more curious and closer to God. Perhaps even let these stories inspire you to ask God, *"What's my story?"*

May the simple question *"Would you be willing to share your story?"* be deeply planted in *your* heart, as if Jesus himself was inviting you because I believe He is!

Todd Miechiels
3/15/20

THE EMPTY ILLUSION OF CONTROL

By Chris Hornsby

If you had asked me when I was a child, I would have told you I was a Christian. From the outside looking in, you definitely would have believed me. Looking back, it's pretty clear I didn't understand what being a Christian meant.

Throughout grade school all the way into high school, I always wanted to do the right thing. I got older and my need for the acceptance of my peers grew so strong I found it easier and easier to walk away from God in search of acceptance. I viewed God as this big, giant God in the sky who came with all of these rules, obligations, and requirements. To a young guy, that came across to me as no fun whatsoever. I always kept my eyes on the other side of the fence of what I thought as the greener grass.

I faked my religious views all the way through college, calling myself a Christian when it would benefit me and totally hiding when the situation would not. That worked for me for so long, I thought, why stop now? That became my life for four years until I became completely exhausted with living a lie. But, I would have still told you I was a Christian if you asked.

After college, I moved out West and I thought I would go to a place where nobody knew me. I could be who I wanted to be. I didn't have to fool anybody or be fake, and that is exactly where I decided to start living for me because I was in control. Living that life almost cost me my life. Drugs became an incredibly important part of who I was. Everything the world offered, I tasted. I found myself doing things I never thought I would do and found myself in places I never thought I would be. Whatever illusion of control I experienced vanished and left me empty. The fact is, all the things that I was chasing to fill that emptiness inside me, those things failed me.

At the time I was waiting tables. I remember it like yesterday. A guest came in and sat down in my section. I immediately recognized him and went over to another server, a good friend excitedly saying, "Hey, did you see who I waited on?"

She said, "No, who?"

I responded, "Man, Michael W. Smith!"

She got this weird expression on her face, then said, *"Who is that?"*

I responded, "Only one of the most famous Christian recording artists in the world today."

Then she showed another strange expression on her face before saying, "Really? Hornsby, how in the *world* would you know that? What are you, a Christian, or something?"

She said it in such a way that it floored me. Her words hit me as though I was sitting in the middle of the interstate with no clothes on and got run over by a Mack truck. In that instant, I remember feeling like, how is it that you have come so far and strayed so far from what you believe to be true; what you grew up knowing as truth, that somebody that has known you for two years of your life , and worked with you every day would not even recognize that you considered yourself a Christian?

I went home that night, laid in bed, and I looked up at the ceiling. I had not talked to God in a couple of years or set foot in a church. Looking up I wondered if my prayers were going to go through the ceiling, and if they did, was God going to listen? Was He going to hear me? Would He even care? I said, "God, if you're there and you love me, get me out of here; just get me out of here because I can't do it on my own." At that point, I felt completely broken.

The very next day, I kid you not, I got a phone call from a family friend. He said he and his father wanted to visit and go skiing with me for a couple of days and asked if I would find them a place to stay.

I knew the father's reputation. He was a sold-out believer of Jesus and a successful businessman. I put down the phone, looked up, and thought, *wow*. I had been running from God for so, so long, and so hard until I got to the end of me. All I did, was knock. I just knocked. I took one step in His direction, and He met me right there. I could not believe it.

We spent those few days together, and God allowed me to see, what I now know were the fruits of the spirit through this man, love, joy, peace, patience, kindness, goodness, gentleness, and self-control. I can tell you 100% when they arrived, I had no joy, no peace, and certainly no self-control. There seemed to be *something* in him absolutely irresistible to me, and I had to have it.

What I have come to find out is that *something* in him was a personal, vibrant relationship with Jesus Christ. God allowed me to be broken, so I could experience the one thing I had never truly grasped or understood, yet now fully aware I did not deserve. *Grace.* The emptiness I had inside me could only be filled with one thing, only one, the love of Jesus.

I decided to put my faith and hope in Jesus Christ, who died for me, gave me the forgiveness I so desperately needed, the acceptance I craved so dearly, and a real relationship with our Heavenly Father. No longer do I want to be known for the things I have done, but rather for what Jesus has done for me.

Watch Chris' story at 315project.com/stories
or point your phone's camera at this image:

BROKEN BREAD & POURED OUT WINE

By Ginger Jones

Your word is a lamp for my feet, a light on my path.
Psalm 119:105

Hi, my name is Ginger. I am 70 years old. I was married for 43 years. I have four children and 10 grandchildren. Raised in central Florida in a middle-class home, I did not experience pain or tragedy, but neither did I experience joy or a sense of purpose. As an extremely rebellious teenager, I entered my 20s, lost, groping around in the dark. I thought I had to figure out everything for myself. I didn't know God. At 24 I married Greg the love of my life, and we quickly had two children. This became God's Kairos moment.

I might need to say a Kairos moment is a perfect time. God's time is always perfect, and this was the perfect time in my life. We decided as suitable parents, we needed to expose our children to God, like you might expose a child to measles. We needed to take our children to church. God took a small opening. I like to say He put His foot in the door and didn't take it out. That was 43 years ago in the spring of 1970. God awakened my spirit, but it would take many years for Him to soften and heal my stony heart.

The journey has been one day at a time. God called me to be His child and that call consists of learning to be broken bread and poured out wine. I say He's called me to be broken bread and think of a grain of wheat. A grain of wheat before it can become bread is required to be ground up and put through the oven and, you can't drink grapes; they have to be crushed and made into wine. That is what my life became, Jesus, making me into His image. His word promises when I stand in front of Him; I'm going to be like Him. I mean, how good is that? He was broken bread and poured out wine, and that's what He calls me to be. My most difficult trial came three years ago when the love of my life died. I like to think of it as him leaving the land of the dying and going to be with Jesus in the land of the living.

The Lord is truly near to those who are crushed in spirit and brokenhearted. He saves them. In the depths of my grief, He gave me a picture of that hope. It's *Song of Songs*, "Who is this coming up from the wilderness, leaning on her beloved?" I knew Jesus would bring me through even this. A year later, I was diagnosed with aggressive breast cancer.

I have walked through the valley of the shadow of death. God showed me, when I walked through the valley, when I walked in a shadow, there appeared to be a great mountain between me and the light. That mountain resembled death. He said, "Fear no evil, for I'm with you."

He is with me and I am His child. I am a delight to His heart. That might be hard for some people who know me to believe, but I am a delight to God's heart.

Mercy holds my left hand and grace holds my right hand, and Jesus is a lamp unto my feet and a light unto my path. Amen.

Watch Ginger's story at 315project.com/stories
or point your phone's camera at this image:

WHO'S REALLY IN CHARGE?

By Scott MacLellan

My name is Scott MacLellan, and I am a disciple of Jesus of Nazareth, who I believe to be the Holy Son of God who came to this earth to die for my sins, was crucified, dead, resurrected, and lives to this day. This is my testimony as to how I came to know.

If you asked me even three or four years ago, if I was lost, I would have said, *"No."* I had a great career, a beautiful wife, and two grown, wonderful daughters. I had a wonderful family growing up, a great school experience, successful in athletics. Though things were going well, if you would have asked me if I were a Christian, I would have said, "Absolutely." If you asked me if I were going to heaven, I would have said, *"Yes."* However, there seemed to be truly little evidence in my life I was a Christian and secretly I had doubts.

Praise God, He pursued me, sometimes in miraculous ways since I was a child. I could spend hours telling you about all the ways He pursued me. I will share two events with you to give you a sense of how much He meant to me and why I have come to know Him.

The first event is two events wrapped in one but separated by 10 years. Now, as some background, my youngest daughter is a three-time cancer survivor, who had two liver transplants, and 150 surgeries in her lifetime. We basically spent the first 18 years of her life in the hospital. One night, many, many years ago, we were in the emergency room at about 3:00 AM. We had been there literally hundreds of times before. This night she appeared to be particularly sick, and she started to code out. Then one nurse turned into three nurses, turned into five nurses, turned into 10 doctors in the room.

In the small room, they kind of nudged me out eventually as they all came in to work on her. I had seen this happen before and had lived through it okay. This night I snapped and turned around to look for anything with a door instead of a curtain. I saw this small bathroom in the emergency room. I ran in there, slammed the door, grabbed the towel off the towel rack, put it up to my mouth, and started screaming into it as loud and as hard as I could. I went on for 10 minutes or so until I had nothing left. I kind of fell back against the wall and slid down to the floor and wept, totally broken, totally bitter, totally lost. With one last gasp of energy, I looked up to God and I said, *"Why won't you let me fix this?"*

What I came to remember was an answer to a prayer that came 10 years earlier with my oldest daughter. I had been at the hospital and came home to clean up and was shaving and getting ready for work. My oldest came into the bathroom where I was shaving. Only three years old at the time, she sat next to me on the tub and I could see her reflection in the mirror sitting next to me. We were chatting and giggling. I was putting shaving cream on her face. I went back to shaving and I could see in the mirror, all of a sudden, she got very reflective, and she turned and looked in the mirror, looking at me in my eyes and said, *"Daddy, I chose you."*

I heard many years later back in high school that children choose their parents. They choose the life they want to be born into.

Whether it's true or not, it does not matter because I had always wondered if my children had chosen me. When she said the words, *"I chose you,"* it got my attention.

The razor literally dropped into the sink. I turned in the mirror, looked back at her, and said, *"What love?"* She goes, *"Daddy, I chose you. You were broken and God sent me to fix you."* I had absolutely nothing. I stared at her in the mirror. She got bored with that, I guess because she said goodbye and got up and left. I sat down on the tub and sat there silently for probably 10 or 15 minutes. Then I started to overthink it. What does it mean I am broken? What does it mean she is here to fix me? I would not know the answer to until 10 years later. God knew the answer to my prayer before I did. It was not me who was to fix it, it was God who was to fix it.

Even with miraculous kind of event, I still did not get it until even 10 years after, at a restaurant talking to a friend, Dave. There was something terrible happening in our family's life at the time. I was relaying the experience to him. It was not a dramatic conversation, just kind of updating him on the facts as to what was happening, and we were chatting. Suddenly, he kind of tilts his head, and he looks at me, and he says, "Scott, do you feel guilty about this?" It did not take me a second, I said, "Absolutely. I feel guilty. I am the spiritual leader of my home. I'm responsible for this." Then he looked at me silently for a second and said, "Scott, God never meant for you to feel guilt. That is what Jesus died for."

Dave kept talking, but I did not hear another word he said. I did not hear anything else happening in the restaurant. I did not hear the silverware clanking; I did not hear people talking. Because suddenly, this wave of unconditional love, forgiveness, peace, harmony flowed into me and took over my body. I sat there for probably five minutes; I do not know how long. I finally got up and left. I got out of the restaurant. I went and sat in my car. For the next 20 minutes, that wave of love just did a work in me I could never describe to you in words.

I realized I had either been doing one of two things. Ignoring everything God was doing, trying to tell me who He was *or* trying so hard to be a good Christian that I was trying to earn my way. What I learned that day, and in reflection is what God had been telling me all along. I did not have to *do* anything. I just had to receive his gift of forgiveness and receive the finished work of Jesus Christ.

What I would encourage you to do is if you've been trying to earn your way there, or if you haven't even been thinking about it, is just receive the gift Christ died to give you, let Him work in you, let Him fix you. Then everything good comes. Praise God, and what He has done in me. My prayer is He does it in you too.

Watch Scott's story at 315project.com/stories
or point your phone's camera at this image:

GOD IS GOOD
IN THE DARKEST MOMENTS

By Julie Ann Allen

I grew up in a small town, in a small church, and sang in a small children's church choir. One Sunday evening when I went to choir practice, I was the only one there. Instead of canceling choir rehearsal, the choir director spent the hour teaching me how to conduct using four-four time and three-four time, as if I was leading the congregation in hymns.

I know she just thought she was teaching a little kid how to conduct, but God used the time to seal a call on my heart. I left choir rehearsal knowing God had claimed me, and I knew what I was to do with my life. At twelve, I was baptized. I wanted to be baptized a lot sooner (like age four or five), but my mom made me wait. She wanted to me to be certain that I knew what was going on. Deep in my heart I did know, *I knew.*

Growing up, we had some financial difficulties in my family. God was just always there, no matter what struggles our family had. As a teenager, I had to work during the summers. I worked all the way through college and every time there was a struggle, God was there.

In college, I met Elan. God's absolute best for me. He understood me like no one ever had before, and we were as much friends as we were romantic. Elan supported me in racing bicycles and as I rode in the Olympic trials. He encouraged me to get my master's degrees in both music and theology. He became the spiritual leader in our marriage and our church. When it came time to have a family, he adored his children. He made work sacrifices and hobby sacrifices to be present with us.

On February 22, 2002, he left for work and did not come home. He died in a work-related accident. Left with a seven-year-old daughter and a five-month-old baby boy, my world turned into this colorless, slow motion, painful chaos. Even in the midst of all of that, I knew God was there. He carried me through some of the darkest, most difficult times, and He guided me and provided for me. I could see God's hand in so many places; in the people that came and helped take care of my children; in the church from across town that provided meals for us for a month. God stayed there.

God turned my weeping into joy. He carried me through the darkest hours. He has showed me He is always there when the toughest times come. Because He is always there, *I am never alone.*

For 16 years now, God has been leading, comforting, guiding, and most miraculously, fathering my children. Both of my kids have seen God show up big, time, and time again. Chase is in high school now and CarleeAnn has graduated from college and is married. We know God has been with us every step of the way.

Despite losing a wonderful husband and an amazing father, our home has been filled with love and happiness. We have been blessed beyond measure. The love and the joy fill our house is something that only could come from a loving and gracious God. We are not alone. God is with us and God is faithful.

I just finished my 30th year as a choir teacher. What started out as a selfless act from a choir director in a small church in a small town has become a 30-year-journey of helping people through their hard times and letting people see that there's so much love and joy in our gracious Christ Jesus. Because He lives, I can face tomorrow. Because He lives, all fear is gone. Because I know He holds the future, life is worth living, because He lives.

I know my story is not unique. Everybody goes through hard times and things that take the rug out from underneath of them. I want you to know God is there. You are not alone. I cannot imagine walking the road I've had to walk without God carrying me through it. I know I would not feel the joy and the love my family shares if it had not been for the grace and the love of Christ Jesus filling and infusing our lives. I cannot imagine not knowing that joy and struggling through the things I had to go through. *Feeling alone.*

Everybody needs to know how good God is. Because even in the darkest times, God is *so* good, and He is there. We are not alone, and I hope this story will help you see that the love of Christ is the greatest thing. I can make it through anything because I know I've got God with me.

Watch Julie's story at 315project.com/stories
or point your phone's camera at this image:

IDENTIFYING WITH CHRIST

By Wesley Vaughn

My name is Wesley Vaughn, and I am legally blind. I was raised in a home where performance meant everything. You perform well, you get the approval of mom, dad, and God. I was told and expected to dress up every week and play the part of the normal Christian family and put a foot forward. The messages we heard each week were hellfire and brimstone messages, and so as a child, I remember many, many times almost every week repeating the sinner's prayer because I came to be afraid of an angry God judging me.

I grew up with the same mentality and took it into young adulthood. I carried it with me even to Bible College. In my pride, I even challenged my Bible professors, and whatever they said, I had a better point, or I seemed right, and they were wrong.

I also continued to perform by singing and to win the approval of others, men, and to win their favor. This landed me in a passion play production of the college. I played the Roman Centurion at the cross, night after night, and very graphic, very impact. The last night of the play, I finally came to the realization through the Holy Spirit, my eyes were opened, and I knew for the first time, I became complete in Christ. His sacrifice, His death on the cross, and His

33

powerful resurrection were all I needed to earn the favor and the love of a heavenly father. I received Christ that night and my life changed. My grid of shame and guilt was broken and taken away.

I continued after Bible College. My journey went into full-time ministry. I became an assistant pastor in New Jersey and there I received four of the greatest blessings of my life. I met my beautiful wife Kamari, and we were married, and then we had three amazing children. All appeared good and seemed well. I turned out to be successful, I had a family, but inside, things were still not totally perfect. Had issues I had not addressed, had not come to grips with, a little darkness, still hanging on and needed to come out into the light.

I remember still looking for a leader, a strong leader to guide me because I did not have excellent decision-making skills. I went to a leadership conference and heard a speaker say you need to depend on God, number one, and then number two, you need to identify with Christ for your character, and He would shape you, He would mold you, not following the pattern of this world, but renewing your mind. Really challenged me and went right to my heart through the Holy Spirit, and I knew I had to change.

When I got back, I found a mentor I could come clean with and be real with and felt safe. God led me to confess the areas of my life had gone wrong. I went to my pastor, my leader at the time, I confessed to him and sent our life into a tailspin. I had issues of pride and lust and greed, going on, a secret life nobody else knew about, not even my wife, and it almost cost me my marriage, almost cost me, my family, my kids. It costs me my ministry at the time, and I resigned. We walked away and I felt abandoned. I felt alone. I felt like a failure.

We decided to move, relocate. My wife held onto the promise of Jeremiah 29:11, which says "For I know the plans I have for you, plans not to harm you but plans to give you a hope and a future." She held on for me because my faith appeared pretty much shot at point.

We started trying to rebuild a life and renew along the path. I had daddy issues still, trust issues and a distant God was displeased with me. I came into a time when physically my eyesight started to go blurry. I went to an ER to get it checked out. They found a tumor on the frontal lobe of my brain. It had to be removed. When they went in to do the surgery, they damaged my optic nerve, and I went blind physically.

This made our life a living hell. It was crazy. This was not the life I wanted. I was angry. I screamed at God when nobody was around and I said, "It's not fair." This is not the life we planned, my wife and I, I have teenagers, three teenagers. God, this is not fair. Why me? Why me? In His loving way, He responded. He said, "Why not you?" He said, "My son was sacrificed and went through suffering for you, to redeem you. I love you. I will look out for you. I always have and I always will."

God once again broke through, and He brought amazing people into my life like my good friend, Tim Smith, like my mentors from my men's group, *Dugout*, and many brothers from a *Souly Business,* a men's ministry. All these people have impacted our lives and helped us to get on a path of hope and knowing whatever happens in life, God can work it out for the good.

I still pray for my sight, many people pray for my sight to be given back, and I know God could work a miracle, and He could give me back my sight either through His work of a miracle or through medical treatment of some kind, but it's His choice either way. I do know this, even without sight, I can still have a vision and I can still look to Him as my perfect heavenly father who loves me and who gave His Son for me and the world, for you.

He is the best choice. Jesus said, "I am the light of the world. If you follow me, you will never be in darkness. You will have the light of life." (John 8:12) Choose life today.

Watch Wesley's story at 315project.com/stories
or point your phone's camera at this image:

GOD'S GOODNESS DOES NOT WAIVER

By Stephanie LeBlanc

In 2013, I was living a quiet life with my husband, Christian, and our four kids who were six, four, three, and one on time. On a vacation to visit out-of-state family, my four-year-old daughter, Adelai, spiked a fever in the middle of the night and complained of severe leg pains. After a day of no relief, I took her in for a routine blood test to rule out an infection and is when we learned she had leukemia. When we got the news, I went into complete shock thinking, "This can't be right. My daughter is too young and healthy for such a disease to be in her body." I knew then my faith and what I believed was about to be put to the ultimate test.

Hit with the reality that no matter how hard I strive to do the right things for the right reasons, life ultimately is out of my control. There seemed that nothing I could do to fix this. The only thing I could control came to be my reaction. I could let her diagnosis wreck my faith or I could choose to let it refine me and bring me into a deeper understanding of who God is.

The first night in the emergency room, the oncologist told us they still do not know why kids develop this type of cancer. My husband, without skipping a beat, looked at the doctors and said, "I know exactly why this has happened to our daughter. Whether God decides to miraculously heal her or if He uses modern medicine to heal her or if He chooses to fit to take her, it will be for His glory."

At the moment, I knew this situation would not overtake us. God had given us a clear purpose for it all. We had a choice to make in our perception of who God is and what He was doing. We could focus on the fear of the unknown, or we could choose to focus on Christ, and His blessed hope He controlled working all things together for good. This choice to trust Him became, and still is, a daily battle. It does not come naturally to me.

Though every heartache we faced while watching her go through the two and a half years of painful chemotherapy treatments, I had to cling to what I knew to be true. I realized we were not fighting cancer, but we were fighting an enemy out to rob us of the joy and hope we have in Christ. Isaiah 26:3 tells us: "You keep Him in perfect peace; His mind stays on you because He trusts you." This is where my true comfort and peace came from, keeping my eyes focused on Christ.

I know God's goodness does not waiver with my feelings or emotions. Where I fall apart and lose to grief, He never does. He has been faithful to always point me back to Him and restore my peace. I could have wallowed in the pain and stayed there, but God gave me the strength to choose joy and to teach my children to do the same. With every tear, we cried together and there were many we also got to experience God's redeeming love and joy as well.

Praise God, Adelai has been healthy and cancer-free since 2016. Even if the outcome had been different, I pray we would still have chosen to sing God's praises; we would have said He is good. I know

God is our loving father and confidently believe He is working all things out for our good.

Watch Stephanie's story at 315project.com/stories
or point your phone's camera at this image:

TYPE-A WORKAHOLIC

By Peter Bourke

I am a work in progress. I became a Christian as a teenager through an organization called Young Life, but I didn't know how to make God an integral part of my life. In fact, I compartmentalized God: Prayer before meals and on Sunday mornings was the box I had God in. When I went into the work environment as a young person, a typical Type-A workaholic and highly driven kind of person, work became consuming for me.

In my twenties and thirties I got restless, about my path, and about my purpose. I can remember having these wrestling matches with God saying, "Lord, how can you give me a set of skills and a set of competencies and experiences and expect me to work most of my waking hours doing this thing called work. I will eventually "retire" which, by that time, I'll probably end up having the big heart attack." This did not make a lot of sense to me. In fact, I can remember dreaming: Boy, if I saved enough money; if I worked hard enough; if I got enough of a nest egg; maybe at some point, I could get to the stage where I might be able to retire, and do noble things to have an impact on the Kingdom.

I can remember working for a Fortune 100 company with a lot of responsibilities and traveling the globe. One day I'm having lunch with my friend Dan and mentioned I was contemplating leaving this high-powered workaholic kind of environment. I told him I wanted to try and get some balance and do some noble things for God's kingdom and God's economy.

Dan said, "Well, why don't you go make a move?"

I said, "Honestly, Dan, I'm not sure it's going to work out."

He said, "Peter, it sounds like you're fearful."

I responded, "That's probably a reasonable way to characterize it."

"Well, you know what fear is, right?" He replied.

Whenever anybody who is wise asks you a question like, you know they have the answer, and you should ask. I said, "Well, no Dan, what's fear?"

He said confidently, "Fear is a lack of faith."

That was a defining moment for me, because I knew, I was trying to be in control. I had my fingers on the steering wheel of life, about as firmly gripped as possible. What I realized and what I am continuing to learn as time goes on is, I am not in control, and God is; and God does not want to be compartmentalized. He wants to be a part of every element of my life. In fact, one of my favorite verses is 1 Thessalonians 5:16 and starts with; "Be joyful always." Verse 17 is the one I always struggle with: "Pray continuously." Continuously sounds like an awful lot and then it goes on to say in verse 18 "Give thanks in all circumstances." What it basically says to me is God wants to be a part of every relationship. He wants to be a part of every decision I make. He wants to be a part of my everyday life.

It has been a real awakening for me. As I grow in Him, I continue to be a work in progress. Every day it is a challenge to figure out how to make Him more and more a part of my day, and more and more a part of every decision. When you get there, and when you have those moments where suddenly God becomes pervasive, as opposed to compartmentalized, the Bible promises you will have "a peace that surpasses all understanding" (Philippians 4:7). That's the cool and liberating part for a control-oriented Type-A guy like me. I am not in control. The good news is, God is.

One other verse I'd like to share with you to challenge your thinking and my own is Romans 8:28 "We know in all things, God works for the good of those who love Him and are called according to His purpose". The liberating part of this is, regardless of the circumstances, what the verses tell us is to give it up to God. If we can surrender our will, our issues, and our baggage to Jesus, that is where we get an awesome sense of peace. I pray that you, too, will experience peace.

Watch Peter's story at 315project.com/stories
or point your phone's camera at this image:

MY PRECIOUS 11-YEAR-OLD GIFT

By Paula Kast

I grew up Catholic. I went to a Catholic school, and I went to Mass on Sundays with my family. If you asked me back then if I had a strong faith and if I knew God, I would have said yes for sure. It was not until later in my adult life that I began a relationship with Christ.

I married my husband, Rick at the age of 24 years old. God blessed us with three beautiful children, a son, and two daughters. At the age of 3 my youngest daughter, Jenna, was diagnosed with brain cancer. She battled this disease for eight years through nine surgeries, lots of chemo, and radiation. In 2010, at 11 years old, Jenna lost her battle with cancer. During her courageous fight, I gave my life fully to God.

Jenna was about to have her fifth surgery, and we were devastated her cancer returned. I became filled with anxiety because I could not bear to watch her suffer anymore. I did not have the energy to put on a good face for my children when my heart ached.

Each time Jenna went in for surgery, the doctors reminded us about the risks involved and how delicate the surgery was. Each surgery Jenna would amaze the doctors with how quickly she recovered, so I became numb to those warnings. Though I was very saddened by the girl in the bed next to Jenna's in the ICU.

She was a beautiful young girl about the same age as Jenna. She had been in the hospital for months but was non-responsive. I watched her mother care for her, visit after visit, lovingly braiding her hair, doing her nails, and exercising her legs. I remember thinking to myself, "Lord, I could never do that. I'm not strong enough."

About a week later, while my husband and I were trying to make decisions for our daughter, I found out what happened to the girl. She had a brain tumor like Jenna, and something went wrong during surgery. I was speechless. I felt like the Lord was sending me a message, and I wanted to scream out, "Did you not hear me? I am not strong enough." That evening, I felt broken and at one of my lowest points. I went to the chapel, no one was there that night, and when I knelt to pray, all I could do was cry.

Then suddenly, in the midst of my tears, I was flooded with memories of Jenna's journey and all the miracles we experienced along the way, thinking about all the special friendships we had made. I started imagining all the other children across the world who were suffering like Jenna and their mothers who were hurting like me. I started gaining strength from them. I began to realize how God had been with us through every step of this journey, how He had been with me my entire life. I realized in a much clearer way how God gave His only son, Jesus, to die, so that we could have life.

I could accept the fact that God was in control, and He loved me more than I could understand. I also knew He loved Jenna more than I was even capable of. I am filled with gratitude to God for blessing me with my three children. I became so grateful He chose me to be their mother. If He had given me the choice years back and said, "I have this incredible gift for you, but you can only have her for 11 years," I would have said yes with no hesitation.

I decided that night in the chapel to trust in God's plan for my life, and wherever this journey would take us, I would look for the Lord in everyone I met. I knew that God was with me. I knew He would love and care for my family. I was still scared, and there were a lot of tough times ahead for me after night in the chapel, but I could have never endured them without holding tight to Christ's hand.

During Jenna's illness, our family started a children's charity. The *Jenna Kast Believe in Miracles Foundation* helps other children with life-threatening illnesses. Even though I lacked business experience and nonprofit skills, God blessed me with the ability to help other children like Jenna. He even sent many angels along the way to help me when I needed it the most. As I look back on my life, I can see how God had been speaking to me in so many ways, and I now spend more time listening to Him.

Though I still fall short, and I still grieve and worry, there is peace in my heart. I know I am not alone, and I am loved unconditionally, which is incredible. Having Christ as my Lord and Savior gives me joy that is beyond explanation, and it is a joy I want to share with everyone I know.

Watch Paula's story at 315project.com/stories
or point your phone's camera at this image:

UNCONDITIONAL

By Eric Corona

My name is Eric Corona. I'm a husband, a father, a son, a brother, a friend, but above all these things, I'm a follower of Jesus Christ. I was the second born to my parents while they were still young and in college. They did a phenomenal job raising us in a loving, caring household. Both of them were raised Catholic, so naturally, I went to a Catholic church growing up, and was baptized as a baby. I went to Sunday school, continued to go through the sacraments, but as with a lot of kids, I only went to church because my parents told me to, and I did not pay attention.

I had a good childhood, a lot of fun, a lot of friends, but at 14, my parents went through a pretty ugly divorce. At the same time my older brother and my role model was leaving for college. I began to let myself slip into this dangerous temptation of self-pity. I started feeling sorry for myself and I convinced myself I had somehow received the raw end of this deal. I was supposed to have a perfect life, but someone else screwed it up. I used that as an excuse to start being selfish and doing what I wanted to do.

The next decade of my life was filled with self-centeredness. All through high school and college, I built my identity around popularity, sports, women, parties, drugs and alcohol. Anything, you name it, I went after it full speed. That led to a lot of dangerous behavior, some run-ins with the law, and some serious consequences. At this point in my life, Jesus was barely an afterthought. When He did pop up, I'd push Him back to the corner of my mind so I wouldn't have to deal with the convictions of the lifestyle I lived. Not until after college did I start to understand the need for Christ in my life. I began to feel empty inside and unsatisfied. All of these earthly pleasures I had chased for so long were no longer fulfilling me. I could tell there was something else out there. I just didn't know what. Lucky for me, the Holy Spirit started tugging me back in the right direction.

I was dating my wife Natalie at the time. As our relationship began to get more serious, her parents took a vested interest in me. They started inviting us to church. While I initially went to please them and impress them, I ultimately continued to go because the message started to resonate with me. I wanted to learn more. Over the next couple of years, my in-laws continued to polish and shine me for their daughter. My father-in-law Tut introduced me to one of his closest friends, a guy named Regi Campbell, who would have a huge impact on my life.

Regi had a group I took part in called *Radical Mentoring*, and the experience changed my entire world. A group of eight of us would meet with Regi on a monthly basis to learn more about the personal relationship we can have with Christ. I got to be honest, when I first started the group, I felt hesitant to say the least. My lifestyle completely contradicted what I thought a perfect Christian was supposed to look like. I continued to experience more and started to desire a personal relationship with this perfect Heavenly Father I began learning so much about, but I thought maybe it was too late.

I found myself at a crossroads. I wanted this relationship, but I thought maybe Jesus wouldn't reciprocate. I pushed Him away for so long and I told Him "no" so many times in order to do what I wanted to do. I came to this irrational conclusion I needed to fix myself and be good enough so I could receive God's love. That led to a futile journey of trying to do everything I could to make myself good enough for God. After many, many failed tries I realized the truth about His love. It is unconditional.

On the morning of September 28th, 2013, I went on a retreat with my group and I had a very real conversation with God. I left the group to be alone, to pray and reflect. I started asking God these questions that were on my heart. To my surprise, He gave me answers. Not some fiery bush or some booming voice from the clouds, but I felt a sense of warmth and peace that over-swept me and gave me an understanding of what God was trying to tell me. He shared with me His love for me wasn't dependent on anything I could ever possibly do for Him, but rather on what He has already freely done for me through His Son, Jesus Christ. It turned into one of the most profound and humbling experiences I've ever had.

It is still amazing to me to try and comprehend how this infinitely powerful creator of our universe was so intensely personal, that He would come to me that morning to share with me how much He loved me and that in spite of my sin and my brokenness, how much He loves all of us. That He would sacrifice His only son to forgive us of all of our sins and provide us with eternal life in His kingdom.

Once I understood these truths, a huge weight had been lifted off my shoulders. I gained a sense of peace and comfort and joy, knowing I have always been an intimately loved child of a perfect

Heavenly Father. I'm not even close to the husband, the father, the man I want to be, but I trust in Jesus. I know He is working in me and for me every single day. Jesus is my Lord, my savior, my brother, my friend, and so much more. This is why I put all of my hope in Jesus Christ.

Watch Eric's story at 315project.com/stories
or point your phone's camera at this image:

LORD, I AM YOURS

By Regi Campbell

I'm Regi Campbell and I'm a Christ follower. After the first 13 years of my career at AT&T Information Systems in BellSouth, I found that I was worshiping the wrong God. God decided that He wanted to get my attention and so He created some disruption, or at least allowed some disruption in my life.

My career started to vibrate. My marriage was in trouble, and I realized that the values that had been taught by my parents really were the values that would, could and should sustain me through life. But in my inner man, I was as empty as a soldier's sleeve with an arm gone. On September 19th, 1983, I walked out in the backyard of my house with all those things going on and I said, "Lord, I'm yours." I surrendered to Him and I trusted Him with *me* for the first time in my life.

Things didn't get better immediately. My wife and I had to start over in our marriage. My career ended at AT&T and I ventured out to start my own business. Six months later I ended up being recruited into another business and from that point in time, I don't know that I've ever had a regular job. I've been involved in many startups. Some have been very successful, and others not so successful.

But what changed in my heart from that night was that God started to live and work in me. The peace that I received is inexplicable. I found purpose. I started to search for my purpose, and I found it. I realized that God was in charge of all the outcomes in my life. I don't have to worry about how things are going to turn out. It's just my job to pray, listen, and obey. To do the next right thing that He leads me to do.

My marriage was healed. I started to disciple my kids and teach them about God, have family devotions and engage with their hearts. As time went on, my businesses started to take hold and I tried to be as positive an influence that I could be for Christ in the marketplace.

But first and foremost, the result of, that transaction that happened in the backyard of my house that night, was the transformation that happened in my heart. As I sit here 62 years old, and I look down the road, I'm the happiest, most fulfilled guy that I know. I'm not there yet, I know I've got tons of work to do, to be the man God wants me to be, but I have faced death and I will still face death. I'm not afraid.

I have peace that surpasses all understanding inside my heart. I have meaningful work to do, to try to bring God and the light of Christ into the marketplace and into the lives of the men that I mentor. I'm not the husband I want to be. I'm not the father, or the grandfather that I want to be. I'm a work in progress like the rest. But the peace that I have in my heart, the purpose that I have in my life, all comes from my relationship with Jesus Christ.

I can't tell you how grateful I am that He reached down into history and into my story, redeemed me, saved me, and adopted me into His family.

Watch Regi's story at 315project.com/stories
or point your phone's camera at this image:

Regi was called Home on 1/24/20. Many can witness that Regi finished well and loved God and others deeply. To learn more about Regi and his life in ministry visit www.radicalmentoring.com

THE FREEDOM OF LETTING GO

By Jessica Lalley

I was born in Greenville, South Carolina, and my parents divorced at the age of five. My mom, brother and I moved to Tampa, Florida, and soon after she remarried. Thanks to a loving and extended family, I grew up always going to church and accepted Jesus Christ in my teens at Tampa Bay Community Church.

Young Life became very influential in my high school faith journey, so much so, that I enjoyed an amazing summer camp experience in 1985 and gave my personal testimony at a Young Life fundraiser in the fall. However, I was still steeped in things like being Southern and honoring our family, religion, traditions, and being the daughter of a politician. The words, remember who you are referred to our family name and reputation.

After high school, I decided I was going to go live the big college experience and all that goes with it. I wanted to be free in a worldly way and that resulted in not honoring God or doing anything that pleased Him. Immediately after college, I moved to Chicago to start my career in sales. Now because of my childhood, I became determined to never be dependent on anyone for anything. I never wanted to be at the mercy of anyone for my well-being. This meant anything that involved my job, my income, dating, and relationships. I was going to be in control.

Now at this time, I attended church because it was something you were supposed to do, to be good, and to meet new people. During this time, I met my dear husband Mark. Two years later, we were married and moved to Atlanta. Over the years though I experienced some intense trials with my mom being diagnosed with cancer, and our daughter suffering from a debilitating case of eczema.

During the time I came to the end of myself and realized I could no longer be in control. I felt so helpless not being able to help either one of them. Interestingly though, I became divinely connected to an amazing group of women in small group Bible study, who at the time, I did not realize would be accelerators in my faith journey and prayer intercessors. Through these women, I received love, mentoring, and biblical teaching that set me up for building a much stronger foundation in my faith, and belief in who I was in Christ.

I thank God for these women and their counsel turned out to be invaluable to me during my early marriage and parenting years and continue to be so to this day. I am eternally grateful for them, specifically, my close friends, Marty Chambless, and Sharon Trent. Through the study of God's word, I learned He does not prevent hardships, but God promises to get us through them.

In October 2007 literally, and almost overnight, our daughter's eczema was healed, not 100%, but close. Rashes went away, sleep returned, and our family restored. I believe through the power of the prayer of these women who witnessed our suffering, along with other people, God delivered a miracle to our family.

With each new challenge and trial that I face, I have learned to release my fears and worries to Jesus. I cannot describe to you the overwhelming freedom and joy of doing so. I have been able to witness an amazing transformation in our family and how God has been working through my husband and our two children, and together we are living a more intentional life for Him. After many years of putting my faith and hope in Jesus, I want to shout from the rooftops and share the freedom of putting my faith and hope in Jesus Christ.

Watch Jessica's story at 315project.com/stories
or point your phone's camera at this image:

BABY, I'LL SHOW YOU A BETTER WAY

By Carla Armstrong

I heard it said before the greater your destiny, the harder the journey, and this has been my experience. I knew from an early age I had a calling, but perseverance, overcoming, and struggles would be my story. At the age of five, I was sexually abused which continued until I was eight years old. By the time I was 11, I felt lost and confused, and all I wanted to do was escape. This led to some very destructive behaviors which led to my making a conscious decision as a teenager to serve evil.

At 19 years old, I found myself in Long Beach, California at a gas station, and met a young lady who drove me down to the beach and told me all about Jesus. I know now the lady appeared as one of God's angels in human form, because for the first time in my life, I cried. For the first time in my life, I wanted to live differently. The person I married became angry about my new conviction. Ultimately this led to every bit of self-esteem being torn away from me leaving nothing but an empty shell.

My marriage fell apart and I moved back home to my parents' house with my three children, where I picked up all my old destructive behaviors once again. I spent every day wondering why

God continued to make me live on this planet. Life became a daily struggle to exist, but I had no choice. I had three children that were depending on me for everything and I did not want them to suffer. I honestly did the best I could, but in the back of my mind, I knew I had a greater destiny. I knew God was preparing me for something where I would be able to serve people like me, and build a better foundation for tomorrow.

In 2001, I lost my voice and my ability to talk. I had a horrible stutter. I was in human resources and customer service so my voice was my life. Faced with not being able to make income because I could not talk to people anymore, I felt devastated and that sent shivers through my soul. During that time, I heard God say, "Baby, I can show you a better way." that changed everything. Two years later my journey with Jesus started again. I started researching Him to disprove Him, and to disprove my need for Him. A simple and logical shift happened. I read a book that said, No matter what you think about Jesus, you cannot argue His brief existence, and the way He lived His life changed the face of humanity forever.

At that moment, I agreed to have Jesus be the guiding force in my life and turned my life over to God. Recently, I heard someone say God will show you the mountain top, and then take you down to the valley to work on you. I spent 11 years in the valley. In my darkest moments, I imagined God saying to me, "Baby, do you love your children?" Of course, I would say "yes", and God would say,

"Then know what you would do for them, I would do so much more for you." It was those words that got me through many days.

Today I see how God has prepared me my whole life for me to be of service to God's children and I am truly and profoundly grateful.

Watch Carla's story at 315project.com/stories
or point your phone's camera at this image:

OFF THE RAILS

By Eric Gilbert

I grew up in Memphis, Tennessee in a normal home and rarely attended church, but when I did, it was with my grandma. At 10 years old, I accepted Jesus as my Savior and got baptized. We moved to Mississippi when I turned 13, and I quickly made new friends. We would go hunting, camping, ride four-wheelers, and drank alcohol. In high school, I started to rebel against my parents. I would stay out past curfew sometimes all night and drink a lot. It got so bad my parents decided it would be best if I went to go live with my aunt and uncle in Florida. There I attended community college and got mixed up with the wrong people. I started doing some serious drugs like pills and cocaine. I ended up quitting school and moving back to Mississippi because I had no plan for my life. I could not hold down a job, and all I wanted to do was party.

In 2005, I got introduced to the drug OxyContin. Two years later, I became a full-blown heroin addict. It got so bad I could not even function without getting my next fix every morning. I started pawning things, started stealing money from my parents, and doing whatever I could to get money for my next fix. This went on for about a year and a half. My parents finally caught on and decided something appeared seriously wrong with me.

In 2009, I ended up in jail for 12 days waiting on a bed to go to rehab. When I got there, I was pretty much skin and bones. I did not want to be there. All I wanted to do was get high. One night, about two weeks into rehab, I decided I was sick and tired of living the way I was living. There were a couple of guys who were always studying the Bible, praying, and talking about Jesus. I knew what I had to do. The only thing I could do.

I got down on my hands and knees, and I prayed, "God, save me. I am tired. Just come into my life and save me. I don't know what else to do." From that day forward, I became a different person. I wanted to do bigger and better things. I finally felt like I had a purpose in my life. While in rehab, I started calling a girl named Kelsey, who was my sister's roommate in college. For some crazy reason, she talked to me. We talked on a regular basis pretty much every day. When I got out of rehab, Kelsey and I started dating. Two years later, we were married, and my son John Eric was born and then two years after, my daughter Caroline.

During this whole time, I got a job with my uncle part-time at a construction company he owned and then landed a good full-time job at a utility company. About three years ago, I got invited to attend a class at church that was going through something called *The Journey*. The Journey taught me what it means to have an intimate and abiding relationship with Jesus Christ, how to pray, how to spend time with Him, how to live in Him and live for Him every day. At 10 years old, I accepted Jesus as my Savior, and it took 15 more years to make Him the Lord of my life.

Where I used to run towards drugs to cope with life, now I run to Jesus Christ. He is my strength. He is my savior, and with Him, I can do all things.

Watch Eric's story at 315project.com/stories
or point your phone's camera at this image:

JOY IS NOT THE ABSENCE OF SUFFERING

By Stacy Ray

I grew up in a small town in Missouri. I can't remember a time when Jesus was not my constant companion. I knew what it meant to walk with Him, but not to be carried by Him. In 2004, my husband Mario and I sensed God calling us to be parents. God used that time to teach us that his plan is always greater than our own.

After discovering we were pregnant with our first child, we suffered a miscarriage. I remember feeling confused and sad, yet still hopeful. We had faith God would see us through and bless us with another child, but it turned out I just wasn't healing. A few weeks later, after a rushed visit to my doctor, we learned that I had not had a miscarriage, but rather a molar pregnancy. They rushed me off to surgery because there was a possibility of the growth turning to cancer and spreading to my lungs. The doctors told me complications from the surgery could lead to a hysterectomy.

God was so gracious. No cancer and no hysterectomy needed. Still devastated, this turned out to be one of the roughest times in my life.

I underwent daily, weekly, and monthly tests for cancer for a little over a year, and the doctors cleared me to try and get pregnant.

We received a blessing with Aiden, a beautiful, healthy boy. It was so joyful.

After his first birthday, we felt we should try for another child, and we were blessed once again with Owen, a beautiful boy, but this time not a healthy one. During a doctor's visit, we learned Owen was born with a heart defect that might require open-heart surgery. It took six agonizing weeks for an appointment with a pediatric cardiologist. We asked everyone to pray for healing. Soon, the prayer requests spread and people we never even met were offering to pray for our son.

I wish I could say I handled all of this with grace, but I can't. After the difficulties to have children and now this, there were a lot of tears and a lot of whys. "Why us? Why our son?" The appointment came and Owen was fully healed. Nothing further would need to be done. A few weeks later, after a late-night feeding, I laid in bed, and God whispered on my heart.

On October 23, 2004, I thought I suffered a miscarriage. Four years later to the day, on October 23rd, 2008, our second son was born. On December 4, 2004, I was rushed off to surgery with no certainty of my future. On December 4, 2008, again, four years later to the day, we learned our son was healed of all his heart defects. God took my two worst days, and made them my two best days. He changed my greatest suffering to my greatest joy.

My hope for you is that you will not see God as some distant deity who set the world in motion. He's someone who waits for you to invite Him to be part of your life, to allow Him to work. If you do, He will show you so many miracles along the way.

We are created to be in a relationship with Him, and I want you to feel that relationship, that love.

Watch Stacy's story at 315project.com/stories
or point your phone's camera at this image:

PREACHER'S KID GOES TO JAIL

By Delton de Armas

For approximately four years, my wife was a widow. For four years, my kids were orphans. When I was sent to federal prison, I never could have imagined I would be grateful for it. My name is Delton de Armas. I am a PK, a preacher's kid. This means we were in church every time the doors were open, and most of the time we were the ones who opened the doors.

At 13, I went to a church camp. I remember singing a song, Jesus, Jesus, Lord To Me. I felt this longing to surrender, to give up control, to make Him Lord, and that is what I did, I surrendered. I gave my life to Him, and I gave up control.

I was a good kid; I did not rebel or stray far off. I mean I messed up as everybody does, but I would say overall, I remained committed to Him. I married Pam, my high school sweetheart. We had three wonderful kids. I had a great job as a CFO of a mortgage company and, we had a faith family, a body of believers we did life with.

In 2009, I had a feeling of unrest. Something just didn't seem right. Pam and I went to dinner with our pastor Ron and his wife, and I remember saying, "I don't feel like I'm doing enough, enough eternal impact, enough significance." That was on a Saturday. On

Monday, the FBI raided our offices. I remember telling Ron after, "Hey Ron, you'll never guess what happened. The FBI showed up this morning." He said, "Delton, I promise you I didn't pray for that."

Two days later we filed for bankruptcy and laid off 90% of the company. Two months later they asked for my resignation. We lived off my savings, I consulted with some churches, and we decided the next step was seminary. We packed up everything we owned, and we moved to Dallas. About a year or so later, I get a call from my attorney, who I had not heard from him in a while. He said, "Delton, a U.S. Attorney wants to meet with us…" "Okay," I said

We flew to Washington and met with the U.S. attorney. He looked at me and said, "Delton, my boss is putting some pressure on me." He said, "You were the chief financial officer of a financial organization who had financial fraud, so you need to be held responsible." I remember thinking, so what does even look like? 'Held responsible'. As it turns out, what it looked like was a plea agreement. What it looked like it was four years away from my wife and kids.

On July 25th, 2012, I surrendered to the minimum-security camp at the Federal Correctional Complex in Polk, Louisiana. As many guys in my position would do, I gravitated to the chapel. I remember the first Tuesday night, a guy named Gene, a guy I ultimately called a friend, prayed. As we bowed our heads he said, "God, I want to thank you for bringing me to prison 13 years ago. I'm so grateful in all you have done in my life." I remember thinking to myself, grateful? Really? I'm not grateful. I'm a little upset, a little frustrated, a little abandoned, like, 'How could this happen to me?'", but there he was, grateful.

After a while I acclimated. I would not say I was doing great, but I survived. Part of surviving turned meant creating a routine and staying busy, and for me, staying busy meant going to chapel. I remember one time in chapel, the chaplain, Chaplain Baby Teeth we called him, said, "Sin falls into two categories: the sin of self-promotion, pride, and the sin of self-preservation, fear." I heard pride all my life, but fear, fear as a sin. I never thought of fear as a sin.

So right then and there I quietly repented. I said, "God, I don't want to be fearful." then I prayed as David does in Psalm 139. I said, "God reveal any wicked way in me. Show me where I'm fearful." and He did. He said, "Delton, you're afraid of rejection. You are afraid of not measuring up. You're afraid of rocking the boat." on and on, He kept revealing. Every time He'd reveal something to me, I would repent, and I would say, "I'm sorry. I don't want to be fearful." I let it go. I know it sounds cliché, but as I let those sins go and I let the fear go, a weight lifted off my shoulders. I felt free.

About three years later I'm sitting in the chapel again, with some new friends and some strangers. But time it is me praying, "God, I am so grateful you brought me here, and I'm so thankful for all you have done in my life."

I have been home now for about three years. I felt grateful then and I am grateful now. Because God's allowed me to see some things, He is doing with what He did. The story we went through, the pain, the suffering, the loneliness, what we called our 'current unpleasantness,' He's allowing us to recycle. He is allowing us to use it in ministry. He is allowing us to reinvest it back into the Kingdom. What I have come to learn is through all of this, God is faithful, and God is sovereign, and God is good.

Watch Delton's story at 315project.com/stories
or point your phone's camera at this image:

THROUGH MY FATHER'S EYES

By Jill Felts

My name is Jill Felts. I'm wholesome, generous, and I try to see the world through my Father's eyes. I grew up in a generous, loving family where I frequently heard of God, but the name of Jesus was rarely mentioned. I always felt Christ's pull on my life, and there have been miraculous encounters that keep me feeling that way.

When I was 24, I married David. Within our first year of marriage he got ill, and he began to lose a lot of weight. He went to different doctors who ran test after test with no answers. It was very painful to watch my best friend suffer. We had said, "for better or for worse, in sickness and health", and we got sickness right off the bat. Through all of this, he continued his demanding career, and we never prayed through any of it.

Two years after we got married, we moved to Chicago. David was starting grad school and we were ready for a fresh new start. One day, we were walking along Lake Michigan; I turned to David and said, "Wait, we have never prayed about this." Right there, we held hands, and we prayed, and we prayed for answers. The first doctor he went to gave us the answer. David had a bad case of salmonella, the worst the doctor had ever seen. With the right medication, he was on the mend.

But what this really showed us was that we started our marriage without God in the center. That whole experience completely rearranged the way we lived. From here on, we were going to live for Jesus, others, and then ourselves. At age 26, I accepted Jesus Christ as my savior, and we were baptized together. Even now looking back, I realized my faith was in my head, more than in my heart. Even though we were active members of our church and had two wonderful little girls, it was still mostly in my head. But something in my business happened, and my faith in God went from my head, to my heart.

While buying an "over the hill" gift card at a gag gift store for a friend, I looked up and behind the clerk, there were all these crosses. I just kind of stared at them and questioned the marketing integrity of where these crosses were placed. A man next to me said, "What are you looking at?" I kind of snapped out of my stare and said, "The crosses." I didn't want to sound judgmental, so I said, "I design sterling silver jewelry and was noticing the silver." It turns out as we discussed my zipper art line that he was the vice president of new vendor relations for the store, and he invited me to the headquarters to pitch my idea.

I was so excited. This was my big break. I knew my business was taking me somewhere and I could not wait to tell David. That night, when he came home, I danced around the kitchen counter and told him the whole encounter. He just said, "Huh… I want to be there when you tell our Sunday school class how you're going to make your first million." Well, I was defiant. I was going to move forward with this. I could do this, I could do that, and I could change their mission. I, I, I, I.

A few weeks later, in the middle of the night, I woke up in a cold sweat. I ran to my computer down the hall, and I typed out wholesome, generous, father's eyes. These words flew out of my fingertips without any thought. I sat there and I stared at them and I realized God had just given me a blueprint of my soul. If this is the blueprint of my soul, what am I doing going into business with this company?

I wrestled with that for a few days, and then I received a phone call from a woman at the company's headquarters. She said, "There's no reason you need to come up here. You're never going to be raunchy enough." I wanted to laugh and say, "I know! I'm wholesome. I'm generous. I see the world through my father's eyes."

After this encounter, two women affiliated with the *Girl Scouts of America* called, and they asked me to design four zipper pulls for the Girl Scouts. Wholesome, the first word of my blueprint. That's when I realized I needed to create a line of jewelry through my father's eyes with a generous spirit. That is how my company *Compelling Creations* came to be. We encourage, and comfort others and ourselves through inspirational jewelry designs.

I was not living a Colossians 3:23 lifestyle that Paul describes in his letters to the Colossians, "Whatever you do, do it with all your heart as if you're working for the Lord and not for men."

I often listen best to Jesus in the middle of the night, so I want to leave you with a dream that I had. I was standing in the open doorway of an airplane above 10,000 feet, ready to jump, with a parachute on my back. Right as fear started to well up within me, I heard a gentle whisper, "I've got your back." Right then I realized that my tandem jumper was Jesus.

Jesus was literally attached to my back. As we jumped, the parachute was the Holy Spirit, completely enveloping our journey. Jesus is my Savior and my tandem jumper. It is with Him that I live with courage, compassion, and love. Amen.

Watch Jill's story at 315project.com/stories
or point your phone's camera at this image:

BUILDING HIS KINGDOM

By David Pace

Have you ever been driving down the road, or maybe taking a walk in the park and see a homeless person? Most people in the world are quick to judge someone like that. Unfortunately, I was awfully close to being somebody like that. No, I was not ready to make a cardboard sign, but I can tell you I felt the sting and the pain of bankruptcy, and I was three days away from losing my home. It was not too long ago that I had a beautiful life, a beautiful family, a beautiful home, money in the bank, no debt, and a great job. It was all for naught. Unfortunately, I was building my kingdom and not His kingdom.

Money was my God. I followed a deep and dark path of sexual sin and alcohol. God has a funny way of getting our attention sometimes, and He got my attention by unraveling my life piece by piece, item by item, until there was nothing left to rely upon, accept His Son, Jesus Christ. This change started to happen while I saw my mother on her death bed. I was blessed to be there at the time for her last few days. I saw her in an incapacitated state, sit up out of bed, and raise her hands to the sky wide-eyed. I can only imagine what she was seeing in the afterlife, and after a few seconds, she collapsed down and went back to her vegetative state. You see, it was my mother who took me to church every Sunday as a kid. She was the one who took care of me and my sister when my father left; I was 10 years of age at the time.

Close to a year after my mother passing, I was sitting on my front porch, and I was reflecting upon a sermon my pastor had given that day from first Colossians. The premise of the verse was about all things being created by Him and for Him. I was reading a book at the time, *90 Minutes in Heaven, by Don Piper.* The person in this book experienced some tragedy and was wrestling with some things, what he was about, and the state he was in. He was ready to give himself up to God and live for Him. It was at that moment, my cold stone heart cracked open and I accepted Jesus Christ as my savior. The warmth I felt and the love of His arms embracing me, caused tears to roll down my face. It was a very humbling experience.

Today, I live a quite different lifestyle, quite different through Christ. I am a small business owner, a craftsman, you might say. I have the ability and the opportunity to help both a local church here in town, and a national organization, with disaster relief from tornadoes. I have seen firsthand the devastation these storms can create, and I have also heard firsthand the testimony of homeowners and what they have experienced. What I can tell you is these experiences are life-changing, and I have seen the wrath of God and the love of God at the same time.

The Holy Spirit led me to start a ministry, *Helping the Elderly.* We provide home repair for those who cannot afford it. For you see, now I am building His kingdom and not my kingdom.

Maybe you are dealing with some sort of sin in your life. I mentioned before in my testimony I dealt with sexual sin and alcohol. Whatever the sin may be, Christ is there as a guide and a protector. Identify what that sin is, take it to Him, ask for forgiveness, and He will provide it to you. You are still going to sin. The difference is that you have Christ on your side, and He gives you a path to follow. If you do choose to follow the path, He will make you a better father, a better husband, and a better person every day. My worldly possessions may be few, but my heavenly possessions are great. Jesus Christ has saved my life, and He can save your life too.

Watch David's story at 315project.com/stories
or point your phone's camera at this image:

GOD'S LOVE NEVER GIVES UP

By Annette Swanson

I grew up in a Catholic household and attended Catholic school my whole life. When I was young, I loved God. But by eighth grade, I began to doubt if God existed. In high school, I only went to church when I had to, but during that time I had an incredible dream that I have never forgotten.

In this dream, I am in a hotel room with my best friend, and we were terrified of something. Suddenly, we heard a knock on the door. When I opened it, Jesus was there, and I was instantly calmed. When He started to leave, I became panicky and asked Him, "Will you be with me?" He said, "Yes." I asked Him, "When?" and He said, "Always." I asked Him, "Where will I find you?" and He said, "In the little things." I woke with the most amazing sense of peace and reassurance. It didn't make me believe in Jesus, but the dream stayed with me.

In my twenties, I was agnostic, and I wanted nothing to do with religion. A friend in college who was both deaf and blind used to quote scripture to me all the time. He would tell me over and over how much Jesus loves me. I would often ask him to stop preaching to me, but he never did (and he continues to quote scriptures to this day).

At age 30, I began dating Bruce, a wonderful man, and a faithful Christian. As our relationship grew, we argued more and more often about religion. When Bruce proposed, he asked me if I would be willing to put God at the center of our marriage. I was eager to marry Bruce, but much less eager to invite God to the wedding. Thankfully, I agreed, and over time, I came to enjoy going to weekly service. I signed on to sing with our worship team and became an elder at our church.

Within a few short years, Bruce and I were blessed with two baby boys and thrilled beyond belief to be expecting a third baby. At the first ultrasound, I was told our baby had no heartbeat. I couldn't bring myself to have a D&C. For the next three weeks, I waited to miscarry while grieving the whole time.

The birth pain started late one night. Bruce was out of town on business, and I was there alone in a room with my two sleeping young boys. In those excruciating awful hours, I desperately pleaded with God to please breathe life back into our tiny little baby. I knew He could, but I didn't know if He would. Right in the middle of my fear, pain, and grief, I heard the most compassionate voice say, "Rest easy, my child." I knew God wasn't going to give me what I wanted, but He would be everything I needed. He fiercely and tenderly loved me in that dark room holding on tight to my hand.

Nine months later, I had another miscarriage. But eventually, God blessed Bruce and me with two more children, a boy, and a girl. When our daughter was eleven years old, she was diagnosed with a rare and aggressive form of cancer. Her cancer treatments were grueling, and it was so hard to watch our precious little girl go through something so terrible. Each and every day I learned more and more to lean on God and to rest in Him. Like my first miscarriage, God showed me how powerfully present He is with me each and every moment.

When I look back on my life, it scares me to think that I could be gone through this latest hard chapter without Him. I am so thankful that He never stopped calling me and reaching for me, even when I wanted absolutely nothing to do with Him. I have faith that God is for me. His unique kind of love never gives up, goes away, or leaves me alone. He has that same amazing love for each and every single one of us. I invite you to ask Him into your heart today.

Watch Annette's story at 315project.com/stories
or point your phone's camera at this image:

WORDS FROM A GOOD FATHER

By Bart Newman

My story is of a broken little boy who, through Christ, became the adopted son of the living God. I grew up with my parents at war with one another. I remember them fighting and arguing so much, as a little kid, I would go to bed every night and pray to God that somehow, He would stop them from getting divorced. As earnestly as any little kid could, I would cry out to God and ask Him to somehow keep my family together, because I loved them both so much and I did not want to be separated from them.

God did not answer my prayer. The summer after my second grade, my parents got a divorce. I was eight years old and my brother was seven. The divorce wasn't a truce between the parties; it simply became a temporary cessation of hostilities. They did not fight directly with each other as easily because they did not live with each other. They instead fought through my brother and me. When I think back to that time, I remember the constant arguments and stress over lack of money. I remember my mom deeply depressed. I remember my dad drinking too much. I remember my brother being beat down by my critical father. Me? I kept trying to make everybody happy and hold on. As I look back, I can think of very few happy moments or happy memories of being a child.

The war between my parents eventually ended. All wars do. This war, like every war, had casualties, my brother and me. By December of my freshman year of high school, my brother became hospitalized for deep depression. My father abandoned me. He did not reach out to me. He would not seek me out or speak to me. I would reach out to him. I would try to call him. He would maybe answer the phone, listen for a little while, say a couple of words, and hang up on me.

I would write him long letters, pouring out my heart to him, asking him to somehow engage and become my dad again. Those letters went unanswered. I felt completely broken and numb. That's when God kind of took over in my life and started to make me strong in those broken places. A good buddy of mine Robert Tidwell, who grew up in my neighborhood, took me to his church lock-in. At the church lock-in, for the first time in my life, I heard the gospel of Jesus Christ.

The minister said that by trusting in the death and resurrection of Jesus Christ and believing in Him, I could have eternal life with God. When I heard him say that, even though I never grew up in the church, and didn't have much knowledge of God, I knew what He was saying was true. I knew if I believed and put my trust in Jesus, I could have eternal life with Him and I did that night. I came to follow the Lord. I did not know exactly what that meant. As I said, I didn't know much about God, or have much knowledge of God. But in a little church, as a part of lock-in, I began the process of learning the nature of God.

The first thing I learned is, that night I had not just secured my eternity, but I also gained an adopted daddy. That I became an adopted son of the living God. This is a father who does not abandon, does not leave, does not neglect, no matter what. As I learned the nature of God, I learned God is a righteous father. He wants righteousness for His children. He wants purity from His children. But at that point in my life as a freshman in high school, I spent most of my time trying to convince girls to do things with me for selfish reasons. Church challenged me to think differently about that. Church challenged me to seek purity and to pray God would give me a godly girlfriend, and one day a godly wife. I started doing exactly that.

In my sophomore year, there was a girl by the name of Julie Schulte, and I knew she was a believer. I asked her on a date, and she said yes. I took her to church. We went on a date together. After the date, I asked her out again, and she said, no. Apparently, my date at the church was not the most exciting thing to do. But I kept praying God would give me a godly girlfriend and a godly wife.

In my junior year, I still felt it might be Julie so I asked her out again. She said, "no" and that she was happy just being friends. But that was ok; I kept praying God would give me a godly girlfriend, and then a godly wife. In my senior year, I still kind of sure it must be Julie. I asked her friends if maybe she changed her mind and would be willing to date me. They asked her, and she said she was not ready. I went on a few dates with another girl. After going on a few dates with another girl, Julie changed her mind and decided she was ready.

In January of our senior year, we went on our first date. Six and a half years later, she became my wife. I am proud to say on the day of our marriage, we said our vows as virgins. God grew us in our marriage, and individually. He blessed us but we also had trials, and we needed to rely on Him to sustain us.

One of those things that was very hard on our marriage was when I deployed to Baghdad, Iraq, with the army. As an army officer, in January 2005, my unit went to a Baghdad for a year-long tour. This proved to be incredibly difficult, one of the most difficult things I ever did. I was not only leaving my wife, who I loved and relied on, but by that time we had a baby girl, who was eight months old the day I flew out of Fort Bragg to Baghdad. The idea of leaving her, and leaving Julie behind, and going to a very violent place, which is what Iraq was, and not knowing if I would return, created all kinds of pain and conflict for me.

During that year in Iraq, God sustained me. He walked with me and He taught me things. He taught me as if He was telling me, "Bart, you are not special, you are not promised tomorrow, and you were only promised today. Every day you need to be using all your time and effort, your talents, and everything I have given you to make an eternal impact and influence others to do the same." I started grappling with fact and the idea that I might not come home, so I started journaling. I started keeping some thoughts I would want Kate to know, my little girl, if I did not come home.

I was blessed that I did get to come home. Nothing bad happened to me in Iraq. When I got back, I felt convicted that I should take my little journal and turn it into a book. So I did. The book is called, *Because of Baghdad: What a Father Would Say about Life if He Didn't Come Home to Say It.* While a few people have read the book and enjoyed it and been blessed by it, the process of writing it down, and making myself decide what matters in life, and how you get the most out of it, blessed me far more than anybody's ever got from reading it.

I have the incredible knowledge that I have given my kids an eternal gift. One day when they're adolescents, or young adults, or even if I'm gone from this world, they can pick up a book and hear my love for them echo through the pages, as I tell them everything I'd want them to know about this life if I didn't come home to say it. Since coming back from Iraq and writing the book God has grown our family.

Kate, who was eight months when I was my way to Iraq, is now 10. We call her Tater Tot. She also has siblings. She has a brother whose name is Luke, who we call The Fluff. They have a sister who is six, Laila, who we call Princess Tumbleweed and last but certainly not least a baby sister named Elise, who we call Lacy. Our kids are growing up in a different kind of home than the one I grew up in. They are growing not in a home where their parents are at war with each other. Their parents are in peace. Our kids are growing up in a home where they know their mommy and daddy love each other and are a hundred percent devoted to them. Even more importantly, our kids are growing up in a home, whereas much as mommy and daddy love them, they are taught and they know, the God of the universe loves them even more.

When I sum up my story, I have to believe the brokenness I had to go through as a child, was for God's purposes. God needed to teach me that I could rely on Him. He needed to teach me that the ways of this world lead to destruction. Because that's the life my parents led.

At the same time, He is using and allowing me to change my family tree. I am not going to root my family tree in the lies of this world. Instead, I am rooting our family tree in the Word of God. He will grow it and flourish it and bless it. Finally, I am learning every day, more and more, despite my struggles, that even when I fall short, I am an adopted son of the living God. No matter what, He will not leave me, and one day I will be united with Him in paradise, forever.

Watch Bart's story at 315project.com/stories
or point your phone's camera at this image:

BEAUTY OUT OF ASHES

By Kris Castro

Ever since high school I have been an easy-going woman with a passionate zeal for life, and fully capable of tackling any challenge that came my way. Jesus has been my best friend since childhood and has always been at the center of my life.

For decades, I watched the Lord come through for me, pretty much in any situation. Then one day in my late 40s it seemed like God failed me in such a huge way. I began to question everything about His character, and I wondered if I could trust Him ever again.

I experienced a very intense season of injustice, continual false accusations, and oppressive condemnation from someone close to me. I pleaded for the Lord to intervene over and over, but through it all He seemed totally silent and, in that silence,, resentment, anger, and bitterness against the Lord my circumstances took root inside me.

For two years those feelings simmered and boiled daily at various degrees. Then one day, to my complete surprise, my anger turned into a tangible rage. I lost all control really scared myself. It was then I knew I needed help, and I wondered if I would ever find my way back to the easy-going woman I used to be.

The help I found was through *Celebrate Recovery*, a Christian 12-step program that helps people to process their hurts, habits, and hang-ups with the Lord. Celebrate Recovery became my lifeline back to sanity as the Holy Spirit led me through each step of surrender and forgiveness, to a deeper level of recovery and healing.

As I reflect on those years of injustice, emotional pain, and brokenness, I realized something. The betrayal I felt towards God was because I could not imagine why my loving King would allow me to suffer so much for so long. When I finally allowed Jesus to become Almighty King over my entire life, and truly surrender to Him, I realized; a loving King will never override someone's free will, even if it means one of His kids suffers. But what He will do is redeem every painful situation, in His perfect timing.

The Lord brought beauty out of my ashes through a mysterious paradox. Rather than rescuing me, He left me in a very painful and unjust situation in order to grow my faith at a much deeper level than I ever thought possible, which bore more fruit than I ever imagined. Through that paradox, I gained a much deeper understanding of who the Holy Spirit truly is and the more "in tune" with the Holy Spirit I became, the easier it seemed to hear the Lord's voice which provided wisdom and guidance whenever I needed it.

After I completed the 12-step program, the Lord completely surprised me by inviting me on a "crazy" Adventure with Him across the country. The adventure forced me to completely depend on Him, one day at a time, and often one hour at a time, over 3-months and more than 12,000 miles! It became the most amazing experience I ever had, and I never once lacked anything. Money and provision showed up every time I needed it, often in miraculous ways only God could have arranged.

I look back on the last 7 years in awe. If it were not for the intense brokenness I experienced, I never would have attended Celebrate Recovery. The CR tools I learned led to a true state of surrender. True surrender developed new spiritual gifts, and those gifts prepared me for that "crazy" adventure.

If I had never gone on that crazy adventure, I would never have learned how to walk in daily intimacy with the Lord. I never would have experienced a more consistent state of inner peace, and restful calm in the middle of any storm, trusting the Lord with all of my needs and surrendering everything to His perfect will.

I am over 50 now, and despite pretty much everything in my life still being unpredictable, I am experiencing more joy now ever before. How is it possible? It is because I truly found my security in the LORD, not in my finances, not in my stuff, and certainly not in my circumstances.

Psalm 46:10 says, "Be Still and Know I Am God." It is a short verse containing a lot of power. As I live out that verse every day, I stand before the Lord as a faithful warrior and beloved daughter, diligently trusting in His unchangeable character, and doing my best to see all things from God's perspective rather than my own.

Please know you are not reading this story by accident. Regardless of what painful situation you are in now, The Lord is right there with you, even if you cannot feel it, and especially when nothing makes sense, and everything seems unfair. The Lord wants to bring beauty out of your ashes as He did in my life. He needs you to give Him permission to begin the transformation process by surrendering everything to Him.

It is ironic, but I learned the more I give up control, the more freedom I receive. When I let Jesus be in the driver's seat of my entire life, I can confidently wait, resting in the Lord, trusting He is going to help me with any challenges come my way.

Watch Kris' story at 315project.com/stories
or point your phone's camera at this image:

NOT JUST A MAN, BUT A MAN OF GOD

By Lazarus Bruner

My name is Lazarus Bruner Jr. I was raised in Oklahoma City, Oklahoma. My parents divorced when I was three, mainly due to my father having issues with alcohol and abuse. Later on, my mom developed an addiction to drugs and that left me alone in environments that weren't safe. But God sent me an angel in my granny, as I affectionately call her. She took the time to invest in me and helped raise.

I developed the kind of mindset where I just was okay being by myself, playing by myself, and just used to nobody being there for me. There were various people, different family members, like my uncles who came along and raised me, but nobody there consistently outside of my grandmother.

At that time I was just learning about life, seeing these ugly situations, and just kind of having my little young mind try to process things. As I got older, my mom reestablished herself, got back on her feet, met a man, and it just took a turn for the worse. He was an alcoholic, and so I was raised in a household where alcohol was always around. With alcohol comes the abuse, the fighting, the yelling, and the cursing. From fourth grade to my freshman year in college, it was just a nightly occurrence where there was fighting, yelling, cursing, or physical abuse. It got to the point where I would just try to get a good night's sleep so I could wake up and go to school in the morning. I would get up and go to school, like nothing happened and put on this mask of optimism. But it was just a cover-up for the pain and hurt I was.

The bright spot was I began playing sports. I knew that performing well academically got me kudos from other people. So that's what I turned to. I invested my energy into becoming a scholar and an athlete. Really, it was just a process of turning a good thing into a God thing, where I relied heavily upon sports for my identity and the sought solace in the compliments of others. It's how I coped with the things that were occurring on the inside.

But as I got older, it grew to the point where I was successful as an athlete in high school, and successful academically, but there was still something that I needed, a reason, a purpose. One day, in my junior year, I got involved with this Christian organization called *Fellowship of Christian Athletes*. It was great because it was about sports, it was for athletes, but it also integrated faith... They had these different types of events called FCA Game Days where we would go attend a football game at the University of Oklahoma or Oklahoma State University. They would have these rallies beforehand, there would be bands and different people speaking and they would present the gospel, and that's where I clearly heard the gospel of Jesus Christ. Hearing that message gave me a feeling that I couldn't shake. It heard it at just the right moment in my life. I felt the nudging in my inner being to respond to this call. I was in this big auditorium and. I'm like way high up in the seats. I thought about all the reasons not to go, how high I was sitting, how long it would take me to get down to the stage and how people were going to view me. I battled and I wrestled, but in the end, the Holy Spirit won. I walked down and I accepted Jesus Christ as my Lord and Savior at 17 years old.

That gave me hope. That feeling really propelled me into wanting to know more about Jesus Christ, but because I wasn't going to church and wasn't being raised in a Christian household, I didn't have the foundation to grow that relationship. I kind of fell back into my old way of life, really resorting to what I knew, and that was serving myself and being selfish. In college, I continued on with the same behavior, the relationships with females, and just serving myself as a student-athlete. That was a time where I would just really feel this void, like I was just harming myself on the inside. Nobody else knew it, but I got very good at hiding my inner feelings and the turmoil that was occurring inside of me. There were times where I would resort to praying. "All right, God, I need you. I'm feeling low." Then as soon things started to turn around, I was right back to my old ways. I just did not understand how come I couldn't change, how come things couldn't change for the better.

I had to withdraw from college twice due to some unhealthy decisions I made. I was a selfish, immature, little boy that only pacified my pain with the things and people that only perpetuated the destruction of my life, my dreams, and my God-given destiny.

As I look back, there's a verse that comes to mind that helps me frame my story and helps me to make sense of all the things. It's Romans 8:28 "All things work together for the good of those who love the Lord and who are called according to His purpose." I now see that all the things that I went through in my childhood have worked out for my best.

In 2004, I married a beautiful young lady who saw the best in me. It was her love that started to challenge those excuses that I used that resulted from my own unreformed nature. She really challenged me, and I love her dearly for that because it was a wakeup call to show me that either I wanted to be a man, or I wanted to be a man of God. Within a year and a half, we had two sons. So now I had the responsibility as a father to raise two and the opportunity to show them what my father didn't show me. There was a great sense of pride that I took in that, and I still take in that.

As we began to go to church together, I started to get around men who took interest in me, who guided me through various seasons of my life, showing me that men of God who follow Jesus Christ are faithful to their wives. Men who follow Jesus Christ are present fathers for their children. It resonated with me because that was the first time I had been told those things. It allowed me to see that there was a huge difference in being a man, and a man of God. I definitely see how God has had His hand on my life throughout each stage of my life, He's allowed me to do certain things, He's allowed certain things to happen to me that gave me a desire and hunger to read His word, and to learn more about my savior.

It was a constant back and forth battle between my old nature and God's spirit in me. It took me a while to understand that those are two different beings and they oppose each other. Until I began to pour into God's word and really see myself as a new creature, it was very difficult overcome past habits. The more I got in community with other believers, the more I listened to His Word, read His Word, prayed, and started to trust Him in all areas of my life. Even in my hurts and pains and hang-ups I began to grow as a Christian, as a follower of Jesus Christ. He really started to separate me from my old way of life. He even delivered me from the bondage of sexual sin and gave me a new identity.

God has been so patient and loving with me. To know that He loves me unconditionally is so freeing. God never wastes any of our experiences, even the most harmful, the most hurtful, and most painful. God uses it all for His glory. Let me tell you how He used it in my life. That same organization that I gave my life to back when I was 17 years old is now the same organization that I work for now, the *Fellowship of Christian Athletes.* Those experiences growing up I use to connect with youth when as PE teacher and a basketball coach at a private middle school. That has separated me from a lot of other teachers, because I'm able to connect with the kids and give them something that they need because I can identify the circumstances they are dealing with. I can teach them how to process those things so that they can overcome it and at an early age. I've learned how to trust God, and my small story is a part of God's great big story, and that gives me hope.

Watch Lazarus' story at 315project.com/stories
or point your phone's camera at this image:

WHY ME LORD?

By Rachel Sweet

My name is Rachel Sweet, and I am a sinner. I was raised Catholic, and believed in a loving God all my life, but I did not have a personal relationship with Jesus Christ. The darkest yet most glorious times of my life were when my children were born. When I was 25 years old, my son Jake was born two months premature. He weighed two pounds, ten ounces. I remember being scared, confused, and angry. At just two days old, Jake developed a condition where his lungs ruptured, causing air to build up in his chest cavity. They rushed us in for a baptism. He flat lined and was gone for 40 minutes. My husband John and I were terrified. Jake continued to grow stronger, and after 34 days in the neonatal intensive care unit, we were able to bring him home. Through all of this, my reaction was, "Why me, God?"

Three years later, we were blessed with our second son Gregory. I was able to carry him for the full nine months, and I thought we were finally given the healthy baby we deserved. But after birth, Gregory continued to turn blue. They brought in specialists and found that his airway was closed off by 75% due to a birth defect, and only surgery would be able to open it. He was in the NICU for

49 days. When he came home, he required 24-hour care until the trach could be removed.

This was a very dark time in my life. I was angry at God, depressed, not praying, and definitely not looking for God. I believe that we had gone through the storm with our first son, and God should have rewarded me for that. I began to see God in believers who surrounded and held me up, who were there for me and my family. They shared God's word to reassure me, and prayed for me and my family for miracles that I couldn't even hope for.

When Gregory was 10 months old, the ear, nose, and throat doctor performed a routine scope of his throat. They found that his airway had opened up on its own. The trach would be able to come out by the fall. When they finally removed Gregory's trach he was able to laugh, speak, and cry for the first time. After the miracle of Gregory's airway opening, my tune changed. It was no longer, "Why me, God?" an accusation, but "Why me, Lord?" In awe and fear. I no longer said, "What can you do for me, God?" But "What can I do for you?"

I may never know why people have to go through so much, but now I have an assurance in a loving God that is in control and He knows the reasons and the outcomes for every darkness and tragedy. This assurance is so strong that when Gregory was two years old and the doctor suspected he had cancer, I was able to give all my fear and worry to God. Thankfully Gregory did not have cancer.

Jesus has filled me with such joy, peace, and assurance that no matter the circumstances and outcomes, He will always take care of me and my family. I truly have been set free by the love of Jesus Christ.

Watch Rachel's story at 315project.com/stories or point your phone's camera at this image:

CAM'S HEART

By Cari Schall

I was blessed to be raised in a loving Christian home. I can't ever remember not believing in God. My faith has always been a part of my life. I honestly believe the strong foundation of faith, laid by my parents, equipped me to cope with events that would happen later in life. Thankfully, my parents and the church I grew up in taught me God does not cause bad things to happen; He does not punish us with tragedy. We live in a sinful world, and we have free will, so tragedy and suffering will happen, and no one is exempt.

In 1997 a horrific accident rocked my family's world. My five-year-old son, Cam, died in a freak car accident; I was the driver of the car and responsible for it. I don't know how I could ever explain the depth of the pain I experienced, but it's like somebody ripped you open and tore your heart out.

At the time of the accident, my four-year-old daughter Elizabeth was with me, and I was six months pregnant with my third child, Kate. In the days and weeks after the accident, I had no choice but to move forward and function as a mom. I went through the next year numb, going through the motions, and emotionally dead. I know it was the actions and prayers of family, my friends, the community, church members, and even strangers supporting that helped with the healing.

Yes, I blamed God. I yelled at Him, screamed at Him, and argued with Him. In the end, I did come to peace with Him as I realized, there is nothing that can happen in this world that can separate us from His love. Another reason I was able to persevere is that my parents taught and modeled for me there's nothing more powerful than the seed of joy in your soul, which comes from knowing Christ as your savior and having a personal relationship with Him.

Just a few weeks before the accident, Cam's Sunday school teacher asked the class of five-year-olds, "Where does Jesus live?"

Most of them replied, "Jesus lives in heaven."

Cam replied, "Jesus lives in my heart."

We had that quote engraved on his tombstone. One reason the quote means so much to me is because I know in my heart could never have walked through that tragedy if I did not have Christ in my heart as my savior and my rock, I'd be in a padded cell somewhere instead of experiencing a life full of joy.

About four years after the accident, God provided a profound moment of peace for me. It was at the baptism of my youngest child, Danny. While I was expecting Danny, my father was dying of pancreatic cancer. Dad decided it was his goal to meet Danny before he died, so as soon as we could after Danny's birth, we hurried to my parents' house. Their pastor came over, and we baptized Danny at dad's bedside. With our family circled in prayer, I will never forget that special moment as we celebrated the end of my dad's beautiful life and the beginning of a new one.

God's message appeared clear: No matter what happened in my past and what would happen in my future, I would always rest in Him, and know His love and salvation.

I know in my heart it is the love and strength of Jesus that carries us through everything. Not only were we able to survive, but we were able to move forward and live full of joy. Knowing Christ as my savior is the biggest blessing in my life. It is my hope and my prayer all will seek, find, and ultimately accept the incredible gift of His love and His salvation.

Watch Cari's story at 315project.com/stories
or point your phone's camera at this image:

HIDING IN THE DUNGEON

By Eric Smith

When I describe myself as a "9/11 Christian", sometimes I get a blank stare. Let me try to explain as best I can. You see I found myself, before I accepted Jesus as my Lord and savior. I found myself consumed and overwhelmed with my work.

It was back in the summer of 2000 when my wife Laurie, our two kids Amanda and Ryan, and I moved from New Jersey across the river from the World Trade Center, down to Georgia. Boy, it was a great opportunity, a chance to get closer to the family, and a nice promotion at work. After 40 years of the winter I was able to escape the wintry mix. I found once we settled in I kind of went back to the same rut, basically hiding in the 'dungeon'. That's what my wife called our home office in the basement. I found me doing email after email, working a lot, and not spending time with the family.

It was the next summer when Amanda, our daughter, was invited to North Point Community Church, and visited with a friend and had an awesome time, and a wonderful experience. Well, ever since then, Laurie, with both kids in tow would go to North Point and guess what? I was down in my dungeon, more emails, and more work. It did not make a lot of sense at the time, but it seemed like it was what I needed to do. I was just so proud of myself for nothing. I did not spend time with the family. I certainly didn't spend time building a relationship with God.

Well summer faded into fall, and we all remember what happened fall. It was in that bright blue 9/11 sky, and the face of the big city skyline where I came from changed forever. I cannot explain that terrible tragedy, but all through that day, I had this feeling God was trying to get my attention. He was trying to pry me out of the basement. He was trying to unite me back with my family, and He was trying to unite me back to Him and His son Jesus, my savior.

Five days later it was Sunday, 09/16, and guess where I was? Not in the dungeon. I was in the van with my family, in the parking lot of North Point Community Church. It was awesome. I had never seen anything like it. All these people, smile on their faces, walking briskly into the church. There I was kind of stuck in the second-to-last row of the west auditorium. The minute I heard Andy Stanley speak, I just knew he was speaking directly to me. I knew at the same time; I had a lot to learn and I had a lot to confess. But at the same time, there was this comfort. A comfort knowing for the first time, I knew who that someone was to learn from, and who that someone was to confess to. It was like that morning at church my old self had died. There was a gap and a hole in my heart, just wide enough for the Holy Spirit to climb comfortably inside.

That was 12 years ago and ever since then, I cannot get enough. I try to soak up every word in the Bible, books, sermons, and meeting with my small group. I spent two years reading the Bible about three pages a day. I called it my 'Cover to Cover' project. For me, that's what it took, that intensity to fully connect, slowly but surely the mighty and strong God of the Old Testament, with the gentle and loving Jesus in the New Testament. At the same time, I also realized I had to stop. I had to stop trying to live for success, for happiness, and for the satisfaction of this world. Instead, I needed to start sharing. I needed to share the magnificent story of our loving God, totally filled with unconditional love and His son, my savior filled with almighty grace.

I must admit though, there are times I still struggle. There are times I still fall short and there are times am still overwhelmed and consumed by my work. But I take comfort in the fact I have a relationship with God and with Jesus, and God's not finished with me yet. I am no longer hiding. I am here confiding. I am confiding that God's calling in my life has been consistent, persistent, insistent, very personal, and specific. I am here today specifically to declare the purpose of my life is to trust God's loving kindness, and to love and follow Jesus every step of the way.

Watch Eric's story at 315project.com/stories
or point your phone's camera at this image:

GOD MADE ME WHOLE

By Marcus Raven

Whether noon, day, or midnight, in your word I abide, for your Spirit doth lead and quicken my stride.

My name is Marcus Raven, and I'm not ashamed to proclaim that for me to live is Christ, and to die as gain. It hasn't always been that way though. By the time I was 22 years old I had made some terrible choices in my life. I was greedy, impatient, and proud. Nobody could tell me anything. Those choices put me in a pretty bad situation. I had been kicked out of the United States Naval Academy, messing up a $250,000 education. I was court-martialed for theft and ended up spending eight and a half months in the Marine Corps brig at Quantico, Virginia. You would have thought I would have sobered up and learned my lesson, but I didn't. I just got mad at the world.

When I came home, I started drinking and smoking weed on a regular basis. About six months later, the state of Texas charged me with first-class felony aggravated robbery with a deadly weapon. By the time October 1995 rolled around, I was doing whatever I could to just self-medicate and avoid everything that was going on. I was still running a gambling shack, but I had stopped smoking weed because I was out on bond and couldn't afford to get caught, and I was getting drug tested at the job I had. I was still drinking a lot and had just moved into a thousand square-feet, super-duper bachelor pad apartment.

I met a woman the day that I was moving in. We began were spending a lot of time together, including overnights. On one of my off days, we were sleeping in. I heard a voice call my name; it was crazy. It was clear and distinct. There were only two of us in the room and I was the only one awake. I pulled the covers back up over my head. A few moments later I heard the voice again. I sat up and looked at the girl beside me. I knew it wasn't her because she was still asleep. I thought I must be going crazy. I rolled over and pulled the covers up again. Suddenly I found myself thinking about the Old Testament book of Samuel. Fortunately, my mom had gotten me into church when I was in junior high. I had been going to church some, listening to different Bible stories, and the one about God calling to the young Samuel as he slept came to mind. I couldn't shake it.

As I began to drift off again, that story was echoing in my mind. The next time I heard my name I said, "Yes, Lord speak." I heard the voice say, "You know if you die like this, you're going to hell." I said, "Yes, Lord. I know." I knew what I had to do next. I woke up my house guest and told her she had to leave. She looked at me and asked, "What's wrong with you? You look like you've seen a ghost." I just laughed a little bit and said, "Nothing's wrong with me? I'm good. Actually, I'm better than I have been my whole life." She started to gather a few things to leave. I said, "No, you got to get everything. You got to get everything and leave. You got to leave."

As she collected her stuff and got ready to leave, she asked, "Are you going to call me?" I said, "No."

Sliding out of the bed, I reached over into my nightstand and pulled out a study Bible. It was a graduation present from the youth pastor of the church I'd gone to with my mom. I opened it and started reading in the book of Romans. I got to Romans chapter 10, verses 9 and 10. I started confessing my sins, about all the women that I've slept with, the drinking, the stealing, and all the crazy stuff— anything I could think of that I knew wasn't right with God but that I was finding pleasure in. I just started to confess all those things. I closed the Bible, put it back in my nightstand, climbed back in the bed, and went to sleep. It's probably one of the best night's sleep I've ever had in my life.

Waking up a little bit later that day, a Wednesday, I went to church. Fortunately, I'm from a traditional church that still has midweek services. Wednesday nights are prayer and Bible study. I got there during the prayer time and noticed that there weren't any guys my age, just a lot of women, and some old guys offering their prayer requests. Pretty much every prayer request was like "get my son off of drugs; help my son, he's in a penitentiary; help my son, he's in a gang; help my daughter, she's messing around with this guy who's on drugs or who's in a penitentiary or who's in a gang." It felt like almost every prayer request was about me. I couldn't shake the feeling that today was somehow my day.

It got even crazier because I stayed for Bible study. They were in the book of Revelation but the guy who was teaching Revelation was out that week, so there was a substitute and he decided to teach from the book of 1 Corinthians. I think its chapter 6 where it says, "Know ye not that your body is the temple of the Holy Spirit?" It talks about not joining yourself to a harlot but glorifying God with your body. I was like, wow, man, this is it. God is talking to me. He is trying to get my attention. I went back again the next night, and again it was like the preacher was preaching directly to me. Man, I knew it. I just knew I needed to submit my life to Jesus. I then walked down the aisle to the front even though hadn't been any altar call. What had happened that morning two days before in my apartment literally transferred me from death into life.

Unfortunately, things didn't immediately get easier. I still had a court case for aggravated robbery hanging over my head. The first time the DA came to me he said that they would give me 18 years on a plea deal. I was like, there's no way in the world that I want to do 18 years. I would have had to do at least half of that before I even came up for parole. I turned down 18. I knew I was guilty and knew they had enough evidence to convict me, but I turned it down. A few months later, they came back with another plea agreement for 15. I said no again. Then a few months later, they came back and offered me 12. When I turned down the offer for 12 years, they told me that was the last offer they would put on the table.

Something in me just kept telling me no, don't take it. A lot of people around me were thinking that I was still in my previous mindset of young, proud, and cocky like I could beat the world. I wasn't. I just didn't have peace of mind about it. In November of 1996, after a lot of prayer and fasting, spending a lot of time alone with God, I decided to go in and plead guilty without a plea agreement. Nobody who knew me or loved me thought that was the right decision to make. But it was like my uncle had told me; I was the only person who had to do the time. I went into a courtroom in Tarrant County, in Fort Worth, Texas, and pled guilty to aggravated robbery with a deadly weapon. It's pretty crazy because the judge could have taken me into custody right there, but for some reason, he didn't. He just looked at the case, looked at the file, looked at me, and said, something's not right here. So instead of taking me into custody as a convicted felon, he let me go. I walked out on the street with no bond to post, no leg monitor, nothing. I just went through a series of interviews. It was crazy.

January rolled around as the DA kept postponing the sentencing date. Then something happened with my lawyer, who was in another trial. The sentencing date was delayed for another six weeks. In early April, I was supposed to go in for sentencing with no plea agreement, nothing. The DA who had offered me 18, then 15, and then 12 saying take it or leave it, that's the last offer you're going to get, postponed things for another three weeks. Finally, on April 28th, the day before my birthday in 1997, I went back to the courthouse. Another lawyer who had joined my team asked me if I would accept the offer of 12 years if it was offered again. I said that I could not do more than 10. He just looked at me like, man, you're crazy, you've already pled guilty, and it's a foregone conclusion that you're going to do time, take the 12. I said, no, I can't do it. The attorneys went off to discuss things.

It seems ironic that through the years my mom has had dreams. She never claimed to be prophetic or anything like that, but she has dreamed about "winning lottery numbers." It's a running joke in our family because if you gave my mom a million dollars, she wouldn't take $1 to play the lottery. But one day I had gone over to her house, and she said, hey, I was dreaming about my lottery numbers and I don't remember all of them, but I sent you to the store to play the lottery and the number was eight. We laughed about it and just chuckled it off. When my attorney came back a few minutes later, he was as white as a ghost. He said, "man, I've been practicing law for over 20 years and I've never seen anything like this. He said a DA had offered an 8-year sentence, take it or leave it." I turned around to my mom and mouthed the word eight. A tear rolled out of her eye, and a tear rolled out of my eye.

The crazy part about it is, the next day; a guy came into the courtroom, almost the exact same case as mine. If you had switched the names on the paperwork, nobody would had ever known. He stood in front of the same judge with the same DA and got 64 years.

One definition of grace is God bestowing blessings on someone who deserves the opposite. At that moment I was the recipient of amazing grace. I knew God was working in my life, and that He was just getting started. I still had to pay the consequences of some pretty riotous living. I ended up spending six years, three months, two weeks, and ten hours in three penal facilities in the state of Texas. While there I was able to minister to other prisoners full time, and I got to see God do some amazing things.

During that time, I had the opportunity to go back to school and get an Associate degree. When I was released, with the help of someone from our church, I was able to continue with and pursue a bachelor's degree. The bachelor's degree opened the door to a good job.

One day, pretty disgruntled at work, I decided to go to the parking lot and call one of my best friends. When I couldn't reach him, I called one of the deacons at my church. He said, "really? I don't know what you're mad about, because you're not in the spot where God wants you to be. You need to finish out." He wanted me to go to seminary so I could get a piece of paper to start full-time ministry. I was very hesitant to do it, but after praying about it and talking to a couple of friends who were doing ministry, I decided to pursue a degree at Dallas Theological Seminary. It was hard, but one of the best things that ever happened to me, happened at Dallas Theological Seminary. That's where I met my wife.

I'm amazed at what God has been doing. I'm amazed that He keeps using me over and over and over again to share His love. He keeps compelling me to enthusiastically show people how gracious and how merciful He is. I get to do it on a daily basis with my wife and my kids. I get to do it at my church, leading a small group. I get to do it on a weekly basis now with two guys from my small group in discipleship. I get to do it when I write poems and create artwork. I get the chance to share with people who do not yet know how amazing Jesus Christ is. I get to tell people who are lost, who are hurting, who are using drugs and alcohol and gambling, and the things I used to do to try to fill a void. I get to tell them that only God, only Jesus, only the power of the Holy Spirit can make you whole. Without Him, I'd be lost. That's why I put my hope in Jesus Christ.

Watch Marcus' story at 315project.com/stories
or point your phone's camera at this image:

HE'S JESUS AND I'M NOT

By Todd Porter

I cannot remember the time before I knew Jesus. I met Him at home through my adoptive parents. When I was three months old, they took me in, accepted me, and loved me as their own. I met Him at church in Sunday school lessons and sermons and music. I met Him in the words of the Bible and in conversations with people of faith.

It is tempting to try to identify a dramatic turning point somewhere along the way, a place you could point to and say, "that's where it happened when everything changed." In reality, it's been a series of moments, one after the other, each presenting an opportunity to move toward God, or turn away from God.

When I hear Jesus say, "Love me with all your heart and with all your mind and with all your strength," I have to face the fact that intellectual acceptance of theological truth, will only take me so far toward wholeness.

So, I start exploring what it means to love God with all my heart and with all my strength. Suddenly I felt like Pinocchio, trying to figure out how to be a real boy that doesn't think the right thoughts about God, but also feels loving feelings and does loving actions.

When I hear Jesus say, "Love your neighbor as yourself," I must face the fact that loving action is so much more than religious activity. I start exploring what it means to love my neighbor. Jesus is a rather good example of loving action, so I start wondering how he lived it out.

He said that He came to bring good news to the poor, release to the captives, sight to the blind, freedom to the oppressed, and proclaim the year of the Lord's favor Luke 4:18-19. I figure if I am following Jesus, then I ought to be able to point to the fruit of provision and release, and healing and freedom are grown as a result. Then I think, well, He's Jesus and I'm well.... not. Here is the thing though: Jesus is not asking us to go do His work for Him, He is asking us to join Him in the work He is already doing. He is not expecting any of us to do these impossible things in our own strength. Instead, God promises to give us what we need to do all He is asking us to do.

I have experienced this provision repeatedly in my life. While I have learned each of these lessons a couple of times, I expect I will learn them a few more times, each time understanding them at a deeper level than the last time. The times when I have made a complete disaster out of things? God promises to make something beautiful out of them.

Wherever you are in your journey of faith, I am begging you: please do not stop there. Keep moving toward the heart of God, who loves you without measure and has hopes for you beyond your wildest dreams. Do not stop until you are living them.

Watch Todd's story at 315project.com/stories
or point your phone's camera at this image:

IS THERE A GOD? YES OR NO?

By Marcus Graham

My name is Marcus Graham and for most of my adult life, I've been spiritually indifferent. I didn't have time for spiritual matters and didn't care about God. When I was growing up, my mom took my three sisters and me to church all the time, but I really didn't get it. What I did get, is that my mom was always praying for us, always praying for me.

After college, I focused on my career, met my soulmate Karen and started a small business. We got married, had three kids, and were living the American dream. When my oldest, Rachel, was four, we started going to church because it seemed like the right thing to do. I kind of believed there was a God, but I still wasn't interested. Fortunately, when Rachel was small, she spent a lot of time with my mom and she learned about God, Jesus, and how to pray. When she was about 11, I recognized that, wow, she's more spiritually mature than was and I felt really awkward about that. I knew that was wrong. I figured I had to decide where I stood on God; Yes, there's a God; or no, there's not a God. Well, as a sales guy, I decided, maybe there's a God? Maybe wasn't going to cut it anymore.

We started going to a new church called North Point and we loved it. It was great. We got plugged into a small group and I shared with everybody that I was having trouble at work. I couldn't meet payroll and was having a lot of struggles. The girl that was leading the group jumped up and said, "Hey, we need to pray for Marcus and Karen, come on." She moved an ottoman into the middle of the room and had us sit on it. I'm thinking, oh gosh, what is this? She had everybody gather around us and put their hands on our shoulders and pray for us for about five minutes. It was an incredible experience. I'd never been through anything like that. I just felt the burden that I was carrying be lifted off my shoulders. I thought, wow, I want more of that. I felt like, yeah, there is a God because He just showed up.

Then a little while later, I met with a buddy of mine who is spiritually discerning, Don Kennedy. He guided me through my final hurdles, and it was at that point I said, "yes. There is a God. I believe, and I'm going to turn my life over to Him." Then Don kind of certified me. He said, "You're in. You're part of the Kingdom now." It was just a phenomenal experience. From that point forward, I was able to really recognize what Jesus did for me and what He was doing for me day in and day out. It was awesome. I can't describe how great it was and it just seems to get better and better. I've learned about patience. I've learned about forgiveness. That was really important for me, how to forgive, and contentment, how to be contented with where I am.

My mom who prayed a million prayers for me passed away in November 2010. But I'm excited to say that she was able to witness her prayers come true when she saw me baptized at North Point on Easter Sunday in 2005. Today, I'm excited to say that I am indeed the spiritual leader of my house. My wife is a wise woman of God. My three kids, Rachel, Kelsey, and Hunter are committed believers. I feel so blessed right now. I'm so excited about my future here on earth and ultimately in heaven with Jesus. I can say proudly that I'm an enthusiastic follower of Jesus Christ.

Watch Marcus' story at 315project.com/stories
or point your phone's camera at this image:

PAIN AS GOD'S MEGAPHONE

By Len Sykes

I heard once if we don't believe the message in the book of Ecclesiastes, we're probably not going to be inclined to read the rest of the Bible. The message in the book of Ecclesiastes, written by King Solomon, is basically this: If we live our lives apart from God and apart from His purposes for our lives, life can become very unfulfilling, even empty, and meaningless.

In 1982, I had an Ecclesiastes experience when I lost my wife and mother of my children to a sudden and tragic death. Suddenly, my life became confusing, empty, and meaningless. Everything that motivated me before no longer motivated me. Many of my friends were motivated by success, money, material things, and having fun, what the world calls 'the good life'. I was having trouble just getting out of bed in the morning.

I knew about the Lord. I had been brought up going to church, but I didn't have a personal relationship with Jesus Christ. The big questions about life began to ring in my ear during this time. Questions like, why did God allow this to happen? and is He good? and does He exist? And why do I exist?" C.S. Lewis puts it this way:

"Pain is God's megaphone to rouse a deaf world. Well, God certainly had my attention."

Before this happened, by God's grace, my wife and I started attending church for the first time in our marriage because it was 'good for the kids.' The people at church reached out to us, served, and loved us, and shared God's word with us. Even with all of that, I was still hurt, angry, and confused, and wondering if God was real or not.

Several months later I attended a retreat. Over that weekend on Saturday night, a friend of mine found a quiet place for us to get away and talk about my struggle with tragedy. She asked me, "Where are you in your relationship with God?" I dumped all my hurt feelings on her, my confusion, anger, and hurt. I told her I didn't know whether or not God existed and asked what kind of God would let something like this happen. Then I said, "I don't know why I exist." She responded by saying, "Len, we're here to praise God and to bring glory to Him." That profound truth hit me because my view of God before this was that He was real, but He was up in Heaven to take care of me, make me happy, and to not let these kinds of things happen in my life.

I'm ashamed to admit how self-focused I was at that point in my life. But God changed me as I realized that night that God created me for His glory, His honor, and His pleasure. As Isaiah the prophet said, "We were formed to proclaim His praise" (Isaiah 43:21).

Later that night we had a worship service and I had a powerful life-changing encounter with the Lord Jesus Christ. I'll never forget that night for the rest of my life. On the way back to Atlanta the next day I began to ask my Christian friends, "How do you get to know Him?" I felt like I had met the most important person in the universe, and I wanted to know Him more deeply, more intimately. Almost 3 decades later, that's still my greatest desire. My passion is to know more Him deeply, more intimately, and to love Him, serve Him, glorify Him, and make Him known to others.

I'd like to ask you, do you know Jesus? Do you know Him personally? I knew about Him. Maybe you know about Him, but you can know Him, personally. He wants you to. He wants you to know Him so much that Jesus Christ died on the cross for all of your sins, so that you and I can have an eternal love relationship with the God of the universe.

Maybe you are like I used to be right now, focused on yourself, and it's time to say, "God, I want to live for you the rest of my life. I want you to come into my life, Jesus, and forgive my sins and change me." He'll do it if you mean it. He did it for me. He'll come into your life and change you from the inside out, day by day until one day you'll see Him face to face. I can hardly wait. Hope to see you there. God bless you.

Watch Len's story at 315project.com/stories
or point your phone's camera at this image:

COMPETING FOR APPROVAL

By David Burkhart

My mom and dad agreed to name me David, after King David from the Old Testament. What they did not agree on was my middle name. My dad wanted it to be Goliath. My name is David Charles Burkhart (thank you, mom).

Born in Wheeling, West Virginia and I grew up right across the river in Bridgeport, Ohio on a hill overlooking the Ohio River Valley. The youngest of seven, I never knew my oldest brother who died two weeks after birth. My dad was a marine in the Korean War and tough as nails. He was more the disciplinarian, while my mom was the nurturing and compassionate one. The church was an important part of our lives. We attended mass every Sunday and I went to Catholic school through the eighth grade. By the age of 10, I felt a need to express myself and started writing poems. Two years later discovered a creative outlet through playing the guitar and writing songs.

As the youngest, I always felt a need to prove myself, and sports seemed like the best way. I wanted to prove to my dad I could be as tough as him, which I wasn't. There is a fine line between toughness and stupidity. My ultra-competitiveness gave rise to many injuries, including multiple concussions from football, and hockey. On top of that, a complete stranger punched me in the face with a glass beer pitcher. I developed debilitating migraines.

During a summer off from college, my brother and I decided to climb down the Grand Canyon with no ropes and no plan. When we split up to find the best way down, I soon found myself hanging by my fingertips off a cliff. Terrified, I made a deal with God that if He saved me from falling to certain death, I would give Him my life. He saved me all right, but I did not hold up my end of the bargain. I became very cynical from watching scandals of high-profile Christian leaders at the time, and decided I wanted no part of institutional religion. From that point, I began looking into new age thinking and Eastern philosophy to find some kind of meaning in life.

After getting my Master's in Communication, I moved to Atlanta to work in cable news. Two years later I met my wife and 10 years after that, we started a family and were blessed with two beautiful boys. Up to this time, competitiveness was my default approach to pretty much everything, and it worked for the most part. I took pride in my accomplishments and wanted others to think my life was perfect. When my youngest boy began a pattern of behavioral problems, I felt like a failure as a father. Then I went into a tailspin when I breached the trust of a friend. My self-image imploded, which set off anxiety attacks and deep depression.

Nine months later, a song about Jesus popped into my head. I shared the song with a Christian coworker and despite my faith not being real at that point; he suggested I enter it into a Christian radio contest. So I did. I didn't win, but all my family and friends said it was a wonderful testament to my faith. Now I felt like I was living a lie because I was unsure of what I believed. Now I was forced to ask the big questions, about faith, and God, and heaven, and was Jesus the Son of God? So many other people believed it, people I respected.

While searching for answers, I began reading *The Purpose Driven Life,* and halfway through the book, the Holy Spirit took over, and I was all in. When I caught a glimpse of eternity for the first time, I felt overwhelmed with a sense of joy I never knew existed.

The Holy Spirit began to lead me away from my selfishness, anxiety, and pride. The debilitating depression that ruled my life was replaced with a sense of joy. That joy could only be found through a relationship with Jesus, my Savior. Despite my flaws, and there are many, God pursued me relentlessly. He allowed me to find Him in my suffering. He kept knocking on the door and tapping me on my shoulder through everything, and I believe He is doing that right now with you as well. No matter what you may have done, what darkness or pain you may find yourself in, realize He will never stop pursuing you. As T.S. Elliot wrote, "God whispers in our pleasures, speaks in our conscience, but shouts in our pains. It is His megaphone to rouse a deaf world." Only by releasing my firm grip on life was I able to accept God's generous gift of grace. I had to be willing to be changed by Him. When you are ready, which could be this very moment, say yes. Invite Him into every circumstance and decision of your life, and He will bless you beyond belief.

Watch David's story at 315project.com/stories
or point your phone's camera at this image:

I AM SAVED EVERYDAY

By Byron Foster

I was born in Sandy Springs, Georgia, just outside of Atlanta. Back then it was a Mayberry type community, like on the Andy Griffith show. We all went to the same Baptist church. My parents grew up in The Depression, and they were wonderful loving parents, where work and church was a part of life. They taught me six things as a child: work, work, work, and church, church, church. I own a pin showing six years of perfect attendance at church. I was there, whether I was sick or not. The same was true for my work. I had a horrible job working in downtown Atlanta at the Farmer's Market. I butchered chickens and pigs all day long. It still haunts me, all that work, but I never missed a single day on the job.

While attending a revival service at our church when I was 12 years old, I felt convicted and thought I needed to be saved, so I would not go to hell. I remember my Sunday school teacher came down, and tapped me on the shoulder, and said, "Would you like to go down to be saved?" I ran forward. I knelt at the altar, and I cried, and I cried, and I waited, and I waited for God to save me. I waited for the lightning. I waited for the clap of thunder. But it never came. I finally just became convinced and tired that I needed to get up. I stood up and said, "I am saved, and I want to be baptized." That's the way it was done at the church. From that day forward I often wondered was I saved, and I was never convinced, because of what I experienced and how I experienced it.

When I graduated from high school, I will never forget our high school counselor telling me I was not college material, and he suggested I work at the Rich's department store downtown. That really cut me to the core, and it hurt like hell. I wanted to prove him wrong, and I was determined to do so. After high school, I got into Georgia Tech, and believe me, it was hard. There were many, many times I wanted to quit, and every time I wanted to quit, I remembered my high school counselor, and I would pray, determined to prove him wrong. When I graduated, my first job was in Huntsville, Alabama. I then got married, and later we adopted a child because we were not able to have a child.

I worked as a contractor for NASA working on the lunar landing program. I helped design the Saturn V and worked on the space shuttle. I later worked for the Corps of Engineers and worked on very large civil works projects. My work took me across the United States. It was a wonderful job. I did not go to church for about 10 years. Basically, I burned out, but when our daughter came along, I was determined to bring her up in a church. I started going back to church and I rekindled my faith. For years, I labored against the stereotypes that were applied to me as a child. The religious traditions of my childhood did not make room for the realities I had experienced.

About three years ago, my wife of 48 years left me after struggling with mental illness for over two decades. This caused a lot of pain and strife in my family. But my relationship with God and

143

the friends He placed in my path in my church carried me through. I know Jesus is my savior, my Lord, and my friend because He walked on this earth, and He understands where I am. He has been my friend ever since that day when I was 12 years old. I will always remember what one of my former pastors said to me. She said, "I am saved every day."

Several years ago, I ran into my high school counselor at a church I was attending. I did not hear anything in the church service the whole time, because I was waiting and waiting to go down and see him and knock his head off, because he had hurt me so much. After the service, I went down, ready to talk to him. I introduced myself, and he did not recognize me, it took the wind out of my sails. However, I told him that because of him challenging me when I was a student; I had done very well in life. I do not think I could have done that without Christ in my heart. Ironically, when I retired, my office was in the building that used to be the Rich's department store.

Because of my relationship with Jesus, and despite all my imperfections, God sees me as white as snow. I know I will be with God when I am birthed from this earth into eternity, and I will be there because of what Christ has done for me.

Watch Byron's story at 315project.com/stories
or point your phone's camera at this image:

SEEK AND YE SHALL FIND

By Nandita Barnabas

My paternal grandfather was converted to Christianity as a first-generation Christian. He fell in love with the Bible and was ordained by German missionaries as a minister. My maternal grandfather was adopted by American missionaries. He then got a Ph.D. in philosophy at Harvard and was also an ordained minister. He went back to India where Christianity is only 2% of the population to start a college for poor Christian students who could not afford a college education.

My dad was a physicist by profession and was also an ordained minister. I attended and graduated from a Catholic school in India and, as you can guess, belonged to a church-going family. I have traveled across the globe for education and lived in France before I came to America. I have a Ph.D. and three post-doctorates in cancer diagnostics. Yet, I consider my biggest achievement in life accepting Jesus Christ as my personal savior at the age of 27.

When I lived in France, far away from family and from anything familiar, the only thing that kept me going was reading the Bible, saying my prayers, and trusting in the Lord Jesus Christ, my living savior. I realized my strength and the peace that surpasses all understanding comes from Jesus Christ himself.

I have been married twice. The first time to my high school classmate who was a non-Christian and the love of my life. The second time was a semi-arranged marriage through which I had two beautiful boys. I became a single mother when the boys were five and seven years old. The younger one was born on the autism spectrum. Thankfully, Christ placed people in my life that provided essential information to get my son the early childhood intervention he needed. Christ stood by us through thick and thin and carried us through. Today, you would not even guess my son is on the autism spectrum.

In Matthew chapter 6:25-34, Jesus tells us not to worry. He will carry us through. It reminds me of the poem, Footprints by Mary Stevenson, which tells us Jesus has carried us throughout our lives in good times and in bad. My sons are now 15 and 17 years old. We have all accepted Jesus Christ as our personal savior. He has carried us through exceedingly difficult times through good times and bad. He is the only true living God. He will never leave us or forsake us.

I start my day every morning with inspirational Bible verses that carry me through the whole day. One of my favorites is "Seek and ye shall find; knock and it shall be opened unto you." (Matthew 7:7)

If something I said stirred your heart to gain a deeper understanding of our amazing Savior, Jesus Christ, I urge you to open and read the Bible and find a Bible-based church. Brothers and Sisters, I am a living testimony of the love of Jesus Christ. Amen.

Watch Nandita's story at 315project.com/stories
or point your phone's camera at this image:

EVERYTHING BUT THE MOST IMPORTANT THING

By Joe Colavito

"In his mind, the man plans his course, but the Lord directs his steps." (Proverbs 16:9).

My name is Joe Colavito and that verse from defines my life story. When I look back on my life story, it lives up to my name. Joe Colavito, full of life in Italian. When I look back, I see beautiful memories of my parents, and of my sister Kathy. A childhood filled with family vacations and celebrations of birthdays and home-cooked meals and more time together than any kid deserved. I leveraged that to achieve success on the sporting field and in the classroom, through Penn State and out into the marketplace. Little by little, I climbed the corporate ladder, chasing after success, trying to make my parents proud of me. Until one day, I caught a good life.

In 1999 as we were in the country club celebrating becoming a young partner in a large executive search firm, I kept thinking, if this is a good life, how come it doesn't feel so good? I learned thereafter that I was spiritually bankrupt. I had traded money and success for my faith in God. A friend, Scott Kauffman, stopped me in the driveway. He asked me the question that changed my life. When you

149

are driving down the highway of life, where is Jesus in your car? I had to admit, as I looked him in the eyes, that He was nowhere in the car that I was aware of. I learned the difference between religion and relationship that day. Four months later in March 2000, I dropped to my knees, I asked Jesus to forgive me for wasting the time and the talent and the treasure He had given me.

I asked Him to be my Lord and savior. That is the decision that will define my life. In his mind, a man plans his course, but the Lord directs his steps. The decision has not made me bulletproof. It has not saved me from trials and tribulations. With two teenagers, five kids in total, and a job, and all the things life brings, I still struggle at times, but when I do, I place my hope in Christ. I cast my fears and my challenges at His feet. At that moment, I get a feeling of peace, and joy that comes from the inside and that's what I rest in. I am so thankful God has directed my steps up to this point, and I cannot wait to see where He takes me in the future.

Watch Joe's story at 315project.com/stories
or point your phone's camera at this image:

BROKEN VESSEL

By Paula Wallace

My name is Paula, and I'm a broken vessel of honor. One of the earliest memories I have is being a small child of five years old when I was brutally raped. As a missionary's kid, losing that purity meant that I would never, ever be a vessel of honor for God, and I really wanted to be. Over the years, I was abandoned, rejected, and betrayed by the people I trusted the most. I was told that even God would not want me, that I deserved the abuse and the pain, that it was my fault. I suffered verbal, emotional, physical, sexual, and even spiritual abuse over the years. I started to think that I must have just been designed that way. You know, like a little kid had taken that clay and rolled it up and twisted it into this misshapen vessel that had bumps and holes and couldn't stand straight or hold anything and then thrown it on the ground and broken and shattered it.

I would reach down and try to pick up the pieces of my life and put them back together. I realized that I was never going to be a vessel of honor. I was just a misshapen vessel with cracks and scars. I'd cry out to God for healing, to fix me, for help. He met me in His faithfulness. He came into my life and started healing and redeeming. I reached out for help, and He started giving me that wholeness. But

I would look in the mirror and I would still see that broken vessel that couldn't be used to serve Him.

One day I asked Him, "God, why didn't you just make me a beautiful vessel of honor? That way you could actually use me to minister." He gave me this vision that just completely changed my heart and my perspective. I saw this dark room and there was dirt, and in the corner, rejected and discarded by everybody was this vessel like me, that was broken and misshapen and couldn't hold anything or stand straight. Then these gorgeous, strong golden hands reached down and picked it up and held it. The hands covered it up and it no longer was about the vessel. The hands completely sealed it and covered it.

Then I saw the hands start to tilt the vessel, and this radiant golden liquid poured out of it. I realized deep down in my heart that it was never about me. Whether I was beautiful and flawless, or I was broken and shattered, that the hands just needed to pick me up and hold me. I had to let the hands pick me up, but it wasn't about me anymore. I realized that my value was in the hands that were holding me. It was in the Spirit that was guiding me. It was in the life that was flowing out of me.

That completely changed my perspective, and I started asking God to use me as I was, every bit of brokenness and pain that I'd experienced, every bit of damage and abuse, for Him to let me share that so that His life could pour through me into others, and they would feel the hope and the life and the beauty that only comes from giving ourselves to Him and letting Him hold us and letting Him fix the damage and letting Him pour His life through us. Like Jesus said on the cross, "Father, forgive them for they don't know what they do." (Luke 23:34). I had to decide to let go and forgive them for my own healing, for my own wholeness, so that the damage that they did, I wouldn't take into myself and let it become my life.

Making that decision has freed me up and traded all that weight and all that damage, for hope and life instead. The amazing thing is now, through my ministry *Bloom in the Dark*, I get to share that life and hope with others, and then I get to join hands with other women who've been broken vessels like me. As a broken vessel of honor, working with them, we get to share that life and hope with other broken women, so that they have hope for their futures too.

Watch Paula's story at 315project.com/stories
or point your phone's camera at this image:

A BATTLE OF FAITH

By Andy Gardner

My name is Andy Gardner. I am a human being, a fleshy distractible, weak human being. I grew up a Catholic, went to a Catholic grade school, and went to mass every Sunday, all in all, a good upbringing.

I had some good examples of Christian action in my life. My grandpa, George, for one. He helped with mentally handicapped people, worked at St. Vincent de Paul, went to mass every single day, always had a rosary by him, and was always praying. All in all, a great example for me, but quiet. My whole family was quiet. We didn't talk about our faith. We didn't share our faith much. It was a personal thing for us, not a lot of hugging going on in matters of faith.

For me, growing up with my faith somewhat on a shallow personal level, I began to get off track a little. I found myself at a youth encounter retreat and going in I sensed what was about to happen for some weird reason. As I got to hear other people my age sharing the stories of their faith, I almost got mad. I knew I was fighting it and kind of knew what was going to happen. At the end of the second night, we were given the opportunity to go to the Sacrament of Reconciliation and inside I surrendered. I had given up.

I knew what I wanted to do. But I was terrified of going through with the sacrament, with confessing these sins and getting them off my chest, starting clean. As I stood there, I felt this weight, like there were hands resting on my shoulders. I knew it was Jesus standing behind me, walking with me to take this next step. I went in, confessed my sins, and to this day, that's the only time I've gone to confession standing up that way. I felt Jesus there with me the whole time. The peace I felt from that moment 20 years ago, became a big changing point in my life.

There have been a lot of amazing moments since then that have strengthened my faith and solidified it. My faith isn't all kisses in the sunshine, frolicking through the meadows with birds, singing. My faith is sometimes a battle, with the war already won, mind you, with its ups and downs and challenges. I know my journey's not over until I'm standing there with Jesus in Heaven. I know enough about myself and the times I've been on my game, and really the best I can be, the times I am free from my big, bad reoccurring sins, the times I'm the best father and husband I can be, the times I'm eloquently able to share my faith with someone, those are like out-of-body experiences for me. Those moments aren't me, that's the Holy Spirit and that gives me great hope. St Maximilian Colby once said, *"Life begins to make sense when we recognize and acknowledge God's infinite goodness and our absolute dependence on Him."* When I think about that, it brings me back to the peace I had 20 years ago and pray I will always remember.

Watch Andy's story at 315project.com/stories
or point your phone's camera at this image:

WORKING FOR THE WRONG REASON

By Payton Mayes

Howdy. My name is Payton Mayes and I'm sharing this story on my 37th birthday. I grew up on a small ranch in Coleman, Texas. Growing up on a ranch taught me the importance of hard work. I discovered that if I worked hard, almost anything was possible. Later, I learned that's not the whole truth.

After I graduated from Texas A&M, I moved to New York to work. Wall Street was the last place I thought I'd ever end up. but it was actually a great place for an ambitious young man like me. A place where hard work and perseverance pays off. I really enjoyed working in the city, but I often flew back to Texas to visit family.

One of those trips was to attend my brother's wedding, where I met a beautiful girl, Andrea, who is now my bride. On our first date in February of 2004, we discovered that both of our parents divorced as we were entering high school. Talking to Andrea, I realized how strong she was. I asked her, "How did you get through all that?" She said, "Well, I know Jesus and I go to church." Then she asked, "Payton, do you go to church?" Quite uncomfortable I replied, "No... I believe in God, but I don't go to church." Her response was, "Well, Payton, if this is ever going to work out, that's important to me."

So, I got on board. I found a church in New York called The Journey that several of my friends attended. After my first visit, I said, "Man, this is a completely different experience than what I thought it would be!" What I found so impressive was that they taught the Bible in a thought-provoking, practical way that even a 27-year-old Texan working on Wall Street could get something out of it.

I knew that I wanted God in my life, but I still hadn't come to terms with what it really meant to follow Christ. I thought I was extremely well by all accounts. My life was going much better than planned, but I was working for the wrong reasons: earning money was my primary goal.

It took a sleepless night on an international flight for God to get my attention. I'm on the plane in the middle of the night and was suddenly startled by a very loud banging sound. I looked around and saw everyone else sound asleep, and I'm wondering, how are they sleeping through that noise? I looked over and saw this beverage cart, and I thought it had to be that beverage cart and turbulence making that noise. I asked the flight attendant, "Can you please adjust that cart so it doesn't make all that noise so I can sleep?" She looked at me like I had three heads. She said, "I don't hear anything." I know now that was the Holy Spirit speaking to me saying, "Payton, what are you doing? You're working for the wrong reasons. Earning money is never going to make you happy. If you fully trust me and follow Me, I will take care of everything else."

I thought I was a Christian. I went to church every Sunday. But that night, I realized that I was just going through the motions spiritually. I never fully appreciated what it meant to really follow

Jesus Christ. I never fully grasped that God sacrificed His only Son to die for my sins. I still struggle sometimes, and I continue to make mistakes every day. But I have such joy and peace now that I know, that regardless of what happens, regardless of what storms are raging in my life, I always have Jesus Christ by my side.

My goal each day is to live more like Jesus and to raise my children to know that they have two fathers. I'm blessed to be their earthly father, but even more joy filled to know and see them develop a relationship with their Heavenly Father.

If you're curious about Jesus, and how to have a real relationship with Him, then I encourage you to talk to someone, because I tell you the truth, three years ago, I was clueless. I was going to church, and I was clueless. But through relationships, and experiences, and that night on the airplane, I've talked to many different people who I greatly respect, and they've been real with me. We all struggle, and we're all broken, but we can all be redeemed through Jesus. I truly believe that through Him, we can do all things through Christ who strengthens us, and we can literally change the world, only through His grace.

Watch Payton's story at 315project.com/stories
or point your phone's camera at this image:

WHAT I'VE LEARNED ABOUT NEXT STEPS (SO FAR)

By Todd Miechiels

It was 2010 and I was sitting up in the balcony at Buckhead Church in Atlanta, a campus of North Point Ministries. I'd been attending regularly for almost three years. I gave my life to Christ at age 35, five years earlier. Even though I was desiring to go deeper in my faith walk, I was quite comfortable sitting anonymously in a crowd with the lights down low. You could have called me a consumer more than a participant. The music was great, the sermons were awesome. I was what you might call a baby Christian, at least that's how I felt.

I was not serving, not plugged into a small group, and not connecting with anyone at church. I was not interested in making an impact on others as much as I was of getting fed and being poured into. By the measures that matter I was pretty much just taking and getting away with it. That all changed when Sean Seay, pastor of Athens Church came and preached a sermon entitled "The Man God Wants You to Be." He said, "if you want to be the man God wants you to be, then you've got to take a next step when He gives you a next step." He hammered home in a loving way what hung in the balance when we choose or refuse to take a next step. The impact that decision could have not just in our personal faith walks, but also in our families and in the body of Christ. You've probably heard people tell stories and say, "I felt like *God was speaking just to me through that sermon.*" That was pretty much what I was feeling that Sunday. I felt like God was speaking directly to me through the pastor.

Then Sean did something that I had not experienced before. He called us out, particularly as men, and said, *"I'm going to give every one of you a chance to take a next step, today. In your bulletin, you will find a card. On that card, you will find three next steps with a checkbox next to each one. Choose a box and hand the card to the person you came here with and ask them to hold you accountable."*

As I looked down at the card, I wasn't sure what to expect but it certainly couldn't hurt to look...

Box #1: Accept Christ as your savior.

Box #2: Join a small group.

Box #3: Get baptized.

I had already accepted Christ. With 3 small kids and very little free time, a small group was definitely out. That left one option, to get baptized.

Perhaps by process of elimination, and/or by the Spirit working, I checked the box to get baptized. Did I desire to get baptized? Not really. But did I desire to be the man God wants me to be? Absolutely. My 'flesh'—my natural way of thinking—was non-committal but there was something deep inside of me that was drawn to take a step. Maybe it's because I'd heard that when you take a step towards God, He will run a mile to you. Maybe because I knew full well, I was living safely inside my comfort zone, just scratching the surface, and desired to go deeper spiritually. I really was **not** looking forward to the idea of getting baptized, I figured I'd have to go through some classes and jump through some hoops. Turns out it was far simpler, and far more difficult.

I remember leaving the church that Sunday feeling a sense of joy and a sense of pride. Pride in that I'd actually done *something* even though all I did was check a box. But I knew it was a decision of the heart, an intentional and declared desire to take a next step. I also remember feeling incredibly grateful to have been in church that day to hear that sermon and be challenged in a loving way.

WHAT DID I GET MYSELF INTO?

The next day my wife was kind enough to remind me that I had checked the box to get baptized. That required going to the church website and registering for baptism. When it comes to self-discipline and being held accountable, I have a natural tendency to rebel and resist. But I had checked the box after all, and my wife called me on it so what was I going to do? I didn't want to wimp out on my baby step of obedience, so I ventured to the website, clicked the link that said, *"register for baptism,"* filled out a brief form, and hit the *submit* button. At this point I was getting a little bit cocky realizing *I just took two steps in two days.* Finally, five years since giving my life to Christ, I was actually doing something, anything, that was out of my complacent comfort zone. Oblivious to what I had really just signed up for, a sense of joy and gratitude lingered but very quickly dissipated as the next day I received an email from the baptism coordinator at the church. The email basically said, *"Hey Todd, we're looking forward to baptizing you next month, and we need you to submit your written story in the next two weeks."* At Northpoint when you get baptized, at least back when I was baptized, they ask you (required you) to prepare and write your story, so they can film it, and play it in service right before they submerge you in the water.

You know that rush of anxiety where things start to go dark in your peripheral vision, and everything goes silent? That's what I experienced. It was what I'd call spiritual vertigo. *What did I just get myself into? My story? I don't have a story!* In my entire life growing up in the church every Sunday until about 16, and then returning 20 years later, I did not remember ever hearing anything about having a story much less telling it, or about witnessing or evangelism. Maybe it's because I wasn't really listening and didn't care to. Sharing your testimony was something that Jesus freaks did at college campuses and on street corners and if they were really crazy, door to door. The concept seemed both foreign and repulsive. The realization I was being asked, and essentially required to share my story pretty much caused me to slam on the brakes. The truth was I didn't even really want to get baptized, and I certainly didn't want to share my story. All I really wanted to do was honor the commitment I'd made to God to take a next step. I thought to myself, why did I check the baptism box? *Maybe I should have just joined a small group instead.*

A frantic conversation kicked off inside my head. If you had told me there was a little Todd devil on one shoulder and a little Todd angel on the other, I would have believed you. The devil was winning this argument saying, *"Who do you think you are to share your story?" "Who cares about anything you'd have to say?" "You know people will think you are a fraud, a hypocrite, and a Jesus freak." "You'd better back out of this while you still can."* Meanwhile, the little angel who was trying to get a word in edgewise wasn't very convincing. The best he could come up with was, *"You've already told people you're getting baptized; you don't want to let them down or look like a fool or a coward."* It didn't take long for me to retreat back into my comfort zone, justifying in my own mind all the good reasons why I should back out. I rationalized it by telling myself that I didn't want to somehow dishonor or let down God by sharing my story. I told my wife that I was going to back out, that I wasn't ready, and that perhaps sometime in the future I could always sign up again. Like a well-meaning and loving wife but a poor accountability buddy she said, *"If that's what you want to do then do it."* That answer surprisingly made me a little angry. I guess deep down I was looking for someone to keep me from backing out.

WITH A LITTLE HELP FROM MY FRIENDS

A few years earlier I had begun attending a men's weekend retreat called *Souly Business*, which helps guys connect with each other, Jesus, and their heavenly Father. Through Souly Business I had begun building strong relationships with men who loved me, and more importantly, loved God. A few of these men became and remain mentors and spiritual guides in my life. I reached out to 3 different guys and told them the pickle I'd gotten myself into, and that I was leaning towards backing out. As God usually does, I believe He guided those men who were wired very differently and at various places in their own walks to essentially say the same exact thing. Each of them basically told me, *"Todd, you are making this all about you. You have to get it right in your heart that this has nothing to do with you, it's not for you. It has everything to do with God, it's all about Him and what He's done and is doing for you, in you, and through you. If you can get that right, you'll get through this, if you can't, you might as well back out."*

This wasn't one of those highly complex and difficult decisions where I needed more information or to seek some elusive answer.

This was pretty clear and binary. Was I willing to stop making this about me my thoughts, my feelings, my fears, my desires and turn my heart towards Him to make it about His thoughts, His feelings, His desires, and His will? This decision was probably the most pivotal and transformational step in my life since placing my faith in Christ. I would describe it as some of the most intense spiritual warfare I had ever experienced up to that point in my life. I essentially made a deal with God. *God, I'll do this, but you're going to have to get me through it. I need you to help me come up with the story you want me to share. I can't do it in my own power, but I'll make myself available to you.* I'm not sure what I thought was in it for Him, and I'm pretty sure it's not kosher to make deals with God, but I was desperate. Curiously, there was a sense of peace at that moment of decision and confession. Suddenly, in my mind, all the pressure was off of me, and on Him. I figured that if this went south it would be His fault as long as I did what He directed me to do. Essentially, I made the decision in my heart to trust the process and leave the outcome to God.

CRUNCH TIME

So with about 10 days remaining until my written story was due, I did what every creative person with an undiagnosed case of ADHD who's been labeled an underachiever their entire life does... I procrastinated. I pretty much avoided the whole thing for another week, probably out of some apprehension but likely more so out of rebelling against deadlines and structure, something I'd been doing my entire life (and still do).

One thing (besides God) that finally got me writing my story was the fact that if I didn't get my written story into the baptism team on time, they would bump me from my baptism date. The problem was, by this time I had already invited several close friends and family members to the event. Some of them were not believers and in fact, were pretty vocal atheists. I knew even I couldn't back out and miss the deadline. Sean's words from his sermon *"you never know what hangs in the balance"*, hung over me like a cartoon word bubble.

Two days before my written story was due, I was visiting a friend who lives in a beautiful mountain home up in North Georgia. What a wonderfully serene and perfect place to tune in to God and carve out some time early in the morning and write my story. There I was at 6:00 am, kids and wife blissfully asleep, and me sitting on the porch with a pen and pad, coffee in hand. Just me and God.

After a brief time of prayer, the story pretty much flowed out onto the paper. Partly because of the easy and helpful guidelines the baptism team provided, and I think partly because I had metaphorically and spiritually handed the pen to God as if to say, *"A deal's a deal, give me the story You want me to share."* I didn't really agonize about it or self-censor what I was writing. It felt like I was taking dictation from God. I don't want to over-spiritualize it, but that's what it felt like to me. In less than 30 minutes, the story was essentially finished. Much of that time was spent in reflection and experiencing a worshipful quiet time. I basically just jotted down what He had put on my heart.

As I've experienced countless times in life but am either too dumb or stubborn to learn, the anxiety around writing my story was far worse than actually just doing it. In fact, in writing my story, I experienced what may have been my first genuine quiet time and journaling. It was a beautiful and living encounter of co-laboring with the Holy Spirit. I wouldn't have used those words or thought of it in that way back then. Back then it was kind of a *"whooooa, that was pretty awesome"* sensation. I felt a renewed and deeper level of peace, accomplishment, gratitude, and the presence of God working with me and through me. It was palpable. Best of all, I felt like I had been freed from being self-centered, if only for a few moments, at least in this one area of my life anyway. I believe it was the result of me turning it over to Him and learning a lesson about being more God-centered.

PROGRESS AND PRACTICE

I sent the written story to the baptism team for their approval. They have some guidelines that ensure the stories are not confusing or drawing unnecessary attention to less important details. They only made a few minor tweaks, so that was comforting. Then they reminded me that there would be no written scripts, cue cards, or teleprompters during the filming. I had to memorize and be able to recite my story in front of the camera.

This wasn't a big deal for me at all as I had been in many theatre productions where I had to memorize a lot more lines than this and while it didn't freak me out, I still knew that my tendency would be to procrastinate. I had about two weeks to memorize my story of 350 words, which is only about a minute and a half. That brought back high school flashbacks and night sweats about being on stage and not being able to remember my lines. It wasn't forgetting my lines that caused me to sweat, it was my theatre teacher and my cast mates knowing I had blown off practicing and preparing for the production. The enemy is so crafty and cunning to try and use that to knock me off the path. I don't recall missing or forgetting a line during a theatre performance so why would I be dreaming that I had totally blown it? By this time, I was becoming increasingly aware of the spiritual battle that the apostle Paul describes in Ephesians 6:12 and all the forces intent on keeping me from making it through this process.

The week before filming, I had committed to spend about 20 minutes each day practicing my story. The thought of rehearsing in front of a mirror freaked me out (it always has), but I knew I needed some focal point to practice looking at, as well as to keep me from looking at my script. I enlisted the help of the Weber barbeque grill on my back deck to play the role of the dreaded camera. My neighbors were probably wondering why I was out there each morning talking to my grill.

I broke the story into paragraphs and practiced each day. By the 5th day not only did I not need my script, I kind of felt like a jazz musician who had invested the time to learn and master the scales and licks necessary to not just play, but play with a sense of freedom and purpose.

In the first several years as a born-again Christian, I don't remember ever spending the time or the intentionality to memorize anything, the Creed, bible verses, nothing. Yet, somehow over this one week of memorizing my story, the story God had put in my head, then on paper, found its way into my heart. Looking back, I had my first experience of meditating on and soaking in His words and His presence.

After sitting passively and silently in the back rows of churches for several years, in a period of about two weeks I had gone from not thinking I had a story at all, to truly knowing my story. From not spending any quiet time with God, to intentionally making time with Him. From racing through life to experiencing glimpses of what a dedicated walk with our Heavenly Father could be like. Abiding, trusting, surrendering, committing, enjoying…these were all words I had heard others talk about in their walks but had not understood or experienced personally. I began to appreciate the power and beauty of being encouraged and guided through a process of knowing, writing and memorizing one's story.

LIGHTS. CAMERA. ACTION.

The day of the filming arrived. They didn't really tell us what to expect other than to be ready and prepared. I had been on camera before but not in a long time. Knowing I would be looking directly into a camera lens rather than being interviewed was a little nerve-racking. For the most part, though I was at peace. I put my trust in the process and asked God for a sense of peace and calm. I knew my story, and I knew that the baptism team was ok with it, so all I had to do was go in there and pretend the camera was my grill.

The most nerve-racking part of the day was sitting in the 'practice room.' They sit you down with 3 or 4 other people who are also filming that day and make you share your story, out loud, looking directly into the eyes of a person of your choosing, as if they were the camera. My sense of calm began to unravel as I realized I was going to share my story with another person out loud for the first time in my life.

I did not throw up or pass out, but those feelings of butterflies you get when it's your turn to speak in front of people kicked in. I am so glad that the practice run was part of the process. It made a huge difference that I wasn't telling my story for the first time in front of the camera. I think they know that most people aren't going to have the courage or discipline to practice their story or share it with other people before arriving on the filming date. Guilt, shame, fear, doubt, fear of public speaking, freezing in front of a camera, and talking about Jesus all have a way of being debilitating and very distracting.

In the filming room, they told me we would do as many takes as needed. That helped with the sense of peace but also made me wonder how many takes did they think I was going to need? That triggered a bit of performance anxiety, but they told me to relax, that everything was going to be fine. Hearing that only made matters a little worse as it sounded like something a dentist would say right before starting a root canal. Even though I was thoroughly prepared, I felt extremely exposed, vulnerable, and completely at their mercy. I remember pretty much butchering my first take, running out of breath due to nerves, and talking way too fast. They told me to relax, slow down, breathe deeply, and give it another go. I think the second take was the final one. They may have gone back and asked me to say the last line a few times. I didn't think I had done that great a job, but no one probably ever does. I didn't worry about it and decided to just continue trusting the process.

DUNKED

The day of the baptism arrived. You are instructed to get there a little while before the service, where a well-trained and loving person hands you a t-shirt and some shorts, tells you to change your clothes, and then report back. I had a little flashback anxiety again like being asked to disrobe for a physical exam. By this point though stepping out of my comfort zone, albeit in little tiny steps was becoming the norm.

173

There I was, sitting in a dark backroom behind the baptism pool. I'd watched others be baptized but watching is different from doing. Things got very real, and very personal very quickly. As the worship songs started blaring from the sound system to a room packed with thousands of people, it felt like a countdown clock to getting dunked. My heart started pounding. There was no turning back. *The Cross before me, the world behind me,* was going through my mind as I tried to focus on the worship music instead of the reality of what was about to happen.

They had me step into the baptismal tank which was wonderfully warm. It's a good thing because my knees were already knocking from the thought of having 3,000 people watching my story (which by the way I hadn't seen myself). I couldn't see anyone because of all the lights. I remember clutching the church staffer's arm trusting he'd get me through this awkward but strangely beautiful ritual of being baptized in front of a large congregation. I was trying to soak it all in, no pun intended, when suddenly, there I was, or at least there was my story on two ridiculously large video screens. All I could do was watch it and wait for it to end before being dunked. There are moments in life that absolutely make your body clinch, hands sweat, and stomach feel like it's going to hurl. This could have been one of those moments, but it wasn't. It was surreal. It was as close to an out of body experience as I have ever had, maybe because I was watching myself on the big screens along with thousands of other people. In any case, I'd certainly never put myself out there in such a public, vulnerable, and exposed way. Strangely enough, I experienced peace and comfort beyond understanding. Surrendering to the moment, and knowingly giving up the desire to control the situation was totally and inexplicably freeing.

I vaguely remember the guy who dunked me saying some inspirational and heartfelt words before putting me under the water. I came back up to the sound of clapping and cheering. At that moment I envisioned the angels and heavens celebrating. I felt like I was a witness to an event more than a participant. The next moment, I dried off, changed back into my clothes, and was back in my seat in the balcony wondering what in the world had just happened. There was definitely a sense of *"My God I'm glad that whole thing is over!"* as well as that increasingly familiar feeling of gratitude, peace, and growth. Not a personal performance-based sense of accomplishment, but more like *"Hey look, God is working in me and producing some spiritual fruit."*

BUSINESS AS USUAL

Now that the whole scary but rewarding *"sharing my story"* journey was behind me; things went back to normal as I focused on work. The process and event quickly seemed like a distant memory but an important mile marker in my walk. I'd taken a next step Sean had challenged me to take, and I wasn't thinking a whole lot about what was next.

A few weeks had gone by, and I working in my home office. I received an unexpected package in the mail. It was from the church and included a DVD and handwritten note that said something to the effect of *"It was great baptizing you, we're happy for you, here's a DVD of your story and the baptism."* While it was kind and nice to get that in the mail, there was a sense of finality to it, like the chapter had closed. I had not had the opportunity to watch my story at that point. Even though they played it in service, I wasn't able to process it at the moment. Assuming that I'd hate the way, I looked and sounded on camera, I opened my home office desk drawer, put the DVD in it and closed the drawer, and went right back to work.

I sat at my desk with the proverbial 16 browser tabs open on my computer (typical for us ADHD multi-taskers). One of the tabs I had open was LinkedIn, a social networking platform for the business world. I happened to be on the profile page of one of my friends who I knew to be Christian, a very devout and strong Christian at that. As I began to scan his profile page, I noticed several things. The first thing I noticed was our many common connections, many of which were also Christian, but many who I assumed were not. The second thing I noticed was that his profile listed every skill, talent, award, group, association, interest, a hobby that you could imagine, but nowhere on the page did it make a mention of Jesus, God, faith, or church. I wasn't judging, who was I to judge? This guy is a spiritual giant in the marketplace. He leads small groups, speaks at Christian business gatherings, and is an elder at his church. Here I was a baby Christian whose only item on my spiritual resume was having just survived the near-death experience of discovering and sharing my story. Did this guy feel that it was wise *not* to mix his faith and work?

I began to look at other profile pages of people I knew to be Jesus' followers and noticed that the lack of visibility to things related to faith was not an anomaly but the norm. Men who I looked up to and aspired to follow had no problem mentioning golf, fishing, fraternities, awards, and certifications, but there was a complete absence of anything that would cause anyone to think or even wonder if Jesus played any part in their lives. I'd grown up surrounded by adults who never talked openly about their faith, always keeping it private, but these men were bold in their faith, at least when they were among fellow Christians.

I decided to extract the text from a bunch of their profile pages and compose a "word cloud" to see what it would look like. It confirmed in a graphic representation what I had perceived to be true, that their faith just was not part of their public persona. I didn't give it much more thought at the time other than to think they knew more than I did, and they probably had good reasons for what seemed like an intentional omission.

Then I looked at my own profile page. It too was completely void of any mention or reference to my faith. A mere month earlier I wouldn't have even given it any thought. No one had ever challenged or encouraged me to share my faith. But I had just gone public in a huge way (at least for me it was huge) and I sincerely felt I had done it in a way that was not self-serving, to honor and give thanks to God.

Being an internet marketer, with a curious infatuation for helping cause change and bucking the system, my mind began to spin. I was sitting with a recorded story that was birthed from a place of struggle and surrender and shown one time in a church service. Now it was sitting in my desk drawer, like a light hidden under a bushel. Similarly, my LinkedIn profile was sitting there. It was a forum for sharing with thousands of people whatever I wanted the world to know about me. My LinkedIn page had a link to my website, and another to my blog. I thought about adding a third link to my story that would allow people to access it if they so choose. I could do that but wondered if I *should* do it?

I didn't want people to think I was a religious fanatic and come off preachy. I didn't want people to think I thought I had it all figured out and was somehow better than them. The familiar self-centered questions, fears, and doubts that had plagued me before at the thought of telling my story resurfaced again. But thanks to my recent experience I was able to put those worries aside and ask God if in the same way I had surrendered my pride and fear in writing and filming my story, could I surrender what might happen if I shared my story on LinkedIn for His purposes and His glory? I received a strong sense of peace and affirmation as if God were saying "that would bring me joy."

Like any child desiring the affirmation and affection of their father, it was an easy decision from there. In about 10 minutes I uploaded my video to YouTube and then put a link to it on my LinkedIn profile. It seemed like a perfect compromise, no one could get offended or accuse me of shoving my religious views in their face when they looked at my LinkedIn page, *but* if someone wanted to know my story, they could click on it at their own discretion, in the privacy of their office or home. I wouldn't be there to make them feel awkward. I wouldn't feel awkward. I wouldn't even know someone was watching it, they could turn it off at any time. It was between them and God.

EPIPHANY

I realized at that moment the power of this simple idea: to take a reverent, thoughtful story about Jesus and the impact He's had in my life, and make it available to anyone, anywhere, at any time. God could use it in places and times where I couldn't or wouldn't be received or choose to go. It felt like a lightning bolt epiphany. I realized that so many of the self-professing Christians that I saw on LinkedIn would likely go to their graves having missed the opportunity to discover their story, and have it filmed, so others could hear and see it. Unless their church offered this type of opportunity to know and share their story, there would likely be no other impetus for them to receive the gift and blessing that I had been given.

I began to think about the thousands of co-workers and associates that know the people I know, but likely do not know that they are passionate followers of Christ or *why* they are followers of Christ. Beyond just the workplace context, it seemed entirely probable that the vast majority of these Christians would die without their spouses, kids, relatives, friends, and perhaps even *themselves*, knowing why they placed their hope in Christ.

I wasn't really thinking "oh man, everyone's got to do this" or "this is an incredible idea." It was more like "this is so simple and easy, what a tragedy for someone **not** to have this opportunity or to even know that it exists." A burden was placed on my heart. I resolved to go back to the church and share these new realizations. Surely, they would start giving everyone the opportunity. They knew how to do it, all they had to do was open the process up to people beyond those getting baptized. Doing so, I thought, could change the trajectory of so many people's faith walks, and impact those who would see and hear their stories. I believed we were sitting on a dormant bomb of historic proportions in both discipleship and evangelism and all we needed to do was light the fuse. I was simply going to encourage our pastor to take this simple idea and run with it. My work was almost finished, or so I thought…

To read more of this unfolding adventure visit:
www.315project.com/backstory

3:15 MINISTRY PARTNERS

3:15 Project would like to thank the many people who have generously supported our mission to help Christians know and share their story.

Kenneth and Sara Abele
Juan Afanador
Rodney Agan
Burke Allen
David Anderson
Robert Ardell
Chris Arias
Carla Armstrong
Greg Austin
William Bacot
Scott Bade
Boyd Bailey
Bruce Baird
Darren Bak
Cullen Barbato
Neil Scott-Barbour
Marian Bart
Dan Baumann
Bob Beard
David Beaver
Scott Beaver
Charles and Laurie Bengochea
David Benson
Dawn Berger
Mike Bishop
Colleen Blackwell
Caroline Boccarossa
Matt Boltin
Peter Bourke
Mark Bowling
Jennifer Brommet
Lazarus Bruner Jr.
Kristen Buhrmann

Andy Bullard
Kevin Burke
David Burkhart
Cary Bush
Mark and Sara Butler
John Caldwell
Joseph Campbell
Regi Campbell
Terence Campbell
Nick Carberry
Joel Carlton
Rick Carnett
Gabriel Carreras
Bob and Gigie Carter
Kris Castro
Adam Cathey
Brian Clark
Joe Colavito
Joe Collins
Chris Collinson
Justin Combs
Susan Conley
Rob Consoli
Charles Cooke
Mark Coote
Eric Corona
Alejandra Correa
Paul Cowels
Norm Crider
Robert Crocker
J.M. and Meg Crowley
Carlester Crumpler
Douglas Czark

Jason Dagley
Brett and Heather Davis
Delton de Armas
John Delk
Robert DiCristina
Maureen Dierkes
Pat Dirrim
Dana Dock Pudenz
Travis Dommert
John and Diane Dotson
Terence Dowling
Michael Duffee
Paul and Caroline Egan
Scott Ennis
David and Jill Felts
Toni Fernandez
Beau Fields
John Fiscus
Matthew Focht
Hans Foraker
Robert Formisano
Brett Fortune
Stuart Foster
Carmen Fowler
John Franz
Peter Freissle
Nancy Gamble
Ed Gandia
Andy Gardner
Chris Gatch
Peter and Carole Geiersch
Dan Gerard
Marge Gildner
David and Debra Gilley
Andy Goddard
Alfred Gomez
Jim Gompers
Rusty and Ann Gordon
Douglas Grady
Marcus and Karen Graham

Mark Granger
Larry and Jody Green
Jeannie Greenberg
Robbie Gring
David Grubb
Fred Halfpap
Larry Ham
John Hanger
Mack Hannah
Andrew Hans Jr.
Kevin Harris
Jay Hassell
Jim Hasty
Dan Hayes
Brandon Hayslip
Steve Head
Mike Henry
Robert Henry
Marc Hernandez
Christina Hice
Brian Hill
Wayne and Katherine Hilton
Julie Hixson
Michael Holton
Daniel and Julie Homrich
Amie Hood
Charles Hooper Jr.
Chris Hornsby
Larry and Barbara Hornsby
Jason Hostetter
Jenise Howden
Parker and Alida Hudson
Chris Hunnicutt
Ike Ikokwu
Conn Jackson
Sami Jajeh
Christopher Jensen
Paul Johnson
Warren and Kim Jolly
Ginger Jones

Michael Jones
Brad Jubin
Sarah Kaczmarek
Steve Kaloper
Michael Kanner
Paula Kast
Nicci Kelly
Laura Kent
George Kinyanjui
Bettie Klapthor
Craig Klein
Dave Klepp
Fr. Ben Kosnac
Catherine Kot
Mark Kreikemeier
Jeremie Kubieck
Derek Kuipers
Taz Lake
Marc and Jessica Lalley
George Landolt
Stanton Lanier
Kevin and Ann Latty
Stephanie LeBlanc
Bob and Judy Lewis
David Lilenfeld
Jay Lin
Jenny Lindsay
Ian Locke
Ben Looper
Lisa Luly
Charles and Brooke Lumpkin
Donald and Julie Mabe
Scott MacLellan
Jay Mahanti
Larry Malone
Laura Malone
Kevin and Katherine Malone
Alex Mammen
Lynne Mapel
Thomas Marbut

Mary Martin
Aaron Masih
Steve Mason
Thomas and Karen Mason
Susan Mattingly
Payton and Andrea Mayes
Stokes Mayfield
Charleen McBrayer
Matthew McConnell
David Mccullough
Dan McDade
Nancy McEnroe
Paul McFall
Beth McGaw
Matt and Amy McKernan
Dave McMullen
Caroline Mendez
Todd and Kim Miechiels
Bryan and Shannon Miles
Benj Miller
Dan Miller
Trey and Majorie Miller
John Mills
Billy Mitchell
Lee and Davis Mitchell
Steve Mitchell
Kevin Monroe
David Montgomery
Mark Montgomery
Jason Montoya
Denise Moore
Brent Morris
Mike Morris
Kathy Neumyer
Bart Newman
Sonny Newton
Randy Nobles
Jody Noland
Richard and Sharon Nuckols
Michael O'Neal

Larry Okenson
Paul Oliver
Jim Otwell
David and Melissa Pace
Charlie Paparelli
Chris Patton
Bruce Paulk
Mark Pendleton
Billy Phenix
James and Dorothy Phillips
Jeff Ping
William and Rene Platten
Phillip Pompilio
Todd Porter
John Posey
Brent Potvin
Kenneth Pullis
Les Randall
Robert Rauton
Brent and Lauren Reid
Mike Reinsel
Todd Renner
Neal Reynolds
Fr. John Riccardo
ReAnn Ring
Jim and Melissa Rizer
Daniel Roberts
Lance Rodgers
Tim Rolston
Edward Rooks
Jim and Mary Rose
Tara Rounds
Emory and Suzana Rowland
Peter and Lynn Ruppe
Carolyn Ruzinsky
Mike Saad
Casey Sanders
Cari Schall
Byron and Linda Schoepf
Steve Schroeder

Tom Schulte
Sean Seay
Mark Shattuck
Kevin and Diana Shaw
Regina Simony
Tim Simounet
Josh Sims
Eric Smith
Scott Smith
Tut Smith
Todd Sorenson
Douglas Spada
Michelle Stahl
Tom Stanfill
Bill Stark
Erich Starrett
Linda Stevens
Jed Strange
Rachel Sweet
T Swezey
Len and Kristen Sykes
Daniel Taylor
Kevin Taylor
Steve Taylor
Greg Teffertiller
Jay Thompson
Suzanne Travers
Jamie Turner
Mike Turner
Wesley Vaughn
Mark Vigoroso
Angie Vittur
Max Wagerman
Randy Walton
Russ and Danielle West
Jeff White
Wade White
Fritz Wiese
John Wiggers
Sam Wilhoit

Andy Williams
Bill Williams
Jim Williams
Loretta Willis
Jack Willyerd
Andy Wilson
Walt Wilson
John Winstanley
Elizabeth Wolfe
David Woodward
Scotland and Margaret Wright
Kris Yankee
Briarlake Baptist Church
Brightmill
Buckhead Church
CBMC Atlanta
Central Church, Memphis
Cloud Walk Ministries
CoreVu LLC
Development Services Group
Dunwoody Baptist Church
Eagle Universal Services
Emily Lorraine Dell Memorial
First Baptist Cumming
First Friday Inc
Fishers of Men
Friendly Human
Global Media Outreach
Gogo Mosquito
Grace Fellowship
High Tech Ministries
iBlast Communications
Jackson Family Foundation
Johnson Ferry Baptist
Linda S Tyler Living Trust

Living Hope EPC
National Christian Foundation
Network for Good
Novologic
Radical Mentoring
ROI Ministry
Roswell UMC
Shepherd's Loft
Simpsonwood UMC
Souly Business
SS Cyril & Methodius
Storyology, Inc
TRU
Utilities Analyses, Inc
White's Chapel UMC
Zoe City Church

IN HONOR OF
Berto Armstrong Sr.
Greg Davis
George and Ora Graham
Karen Kennedy
Todd Miechiels
Laurie Smith
Jonathan Vaughn
Jordan Vaughn
Joshua Vaughn

IN MEMORY OF
Brenda Ann Armstrong
Mary Helen Bennett Long
Regi Campbell
Mary Drayton Godbee
Betty Peleske Schulte
Larue Norris

RESOURCES

EVERYONE HAS A STORY

A Devotional by Boyd Bailey

If someone else thinks they have reasons to put confidence in the flesh, I have more: circumcised on the eighth day, of the people of Israel, of the tribe of Benjamin, a Hebrew of Hebrews; in regard to the law, a Pharisee; as for zeal, persecuting the church; as for righteousness based on the law, faultless. But whatever were gains to me I now consider loss for the sake of Christ. (Philippines 3:4-7)

Everyone has a story. Maybe your story is similar to mine. A story of my parent's divorce at age five followed by confusion, hurt, and blame. A story of insecurity and distrust based on a constant state of transition and multiple moves. Embarrassed by being the new kid in the class, over and over again. A story of a coach who loved Christ and loved his wife, who led Bible studies and encouraged me in my undeveloped faith. At 19, Jesus entered the screenplay of my life as Lord.

Married my high school sweetheart, whose family's faith in God flourished. My bride was and is my best friend. She is also the best wife and mom I know. My father-in-law became my mentor of hard work and how to love my family. Sold my service business, graduated with a Master of Divinity, worked in large churches, started three ministries, and experienced the joy of my Dad's salvation. Blessed with four daughters, three sons-in-law, and four grandbabies. Have survived by God's grace, prostate cancer, abusive stepfathers, rejection, and financial challenges. My story.

I am reminded of your sincere faith, which first lived in your grandmother Lois and in your mother Eunice and, I am persuaded, now lives in you also. (2 Timothy 1:5)

So, each day we look into the eyes of each person the Lord sends our way and we inquire about their story. A rough persona may mask a big, insecure heart. A hyper happy person may be hiding intense hurt that needs the healing touch of God's grace. A fatigued face may have been up most of the night with a special need's child. A sad soul may struggle under a financial burden and a joyful co-worker could use our support and affirmation. Learn another's story.

Above all else, the story of Almighty God's grace, love, and judgment is the main attraction. Our stories are the warmup band, but His story is what others really want and need to hear. When we submit our story to Christ's story our story becomes complete and His story becomes the focal point of our life. His humility becomes our humility. His love becomes our love. His sacrifice becomes our sacrifice. His forgiveness becomes our forgiveness. His story becomes our story.

The very credentials these people are waving around as something special, I'm tearing up and throwing out with the trash—along with everything else I used to take credit for. Why? Because of Christ.

Yes, all the things I once thought were so important are gone from my life. Compared to the high privilege of knowing Christ Jesus as my Master. (Philippians 3:7-9), The Message

Prayer

Heavenly Father, I pray Your story of love and forgiveness becomes my story of love and forgiveness.

Originally published October 2, 2013, at WisdomHunters.com

GO AND TELL

A Devotional by Boyd Bailey

The first thing Andrew did was to find his brother Simon and tell him, "We have found the Messiah" (that is, the Christ). he brought him to Jesus. (John 1:41-42)

Those who experience the abiding joy of Jesus cannot sit still with their new discovery. Lost souls who have seen the love of the Lord forgive their sin, are compelled to love their friends to the Lord. People who once panicked in fear, but now have peace with their heavenly Father, must share with others their hope in Christ. The fullness of the Spirit in a saved soul bids believers to bring people to Jesus. We who know Jesus are called by God to introduce others to Jesus.

You may say, *"I am not a great debater,"* or *"I have limited experience following Christ,"* or God forbid, *"I am not a professional Christian."* See these statements as assets, not liabilities. A knowledge of apologetics is helpful, but not necessary to explain the depth of God's love in (John 3:16). Yes, you have the opportunity to grow your faith with life's ups and downs. But, from the start of salvation, you can tell your story, *"Once I was spiritually blind, but now I see."* Lastly, those in vocational ministry are paid to serve, but you can serve as a grateful and generous volunteer.

"Many of the Samaritans from that town believed in Him because of the woman's testimony, "He told me everything I ever did" (John 4:39).

Once we introduce people to our best friend Jesus, He will invite them unto Himself. The Holy Spirit will reveal the needy heart of the seeker and the holy heart of their Savior Christ Jesus. He initiates irresistible intimacy their soul longs to enjoy. We make the introductions, but the Spirit draws hungry hearts to know Him in a loving relationship for a lifetime. We plant a seed of Scripture, the Spirit waters the Word with conviction, and God harvests the heart for Himself.

Furthermore, be creative with your invitations to Jesus. Invite your family to Easter Sunday and lunch after the church service. Invite a co-worker to a men or women's weekend retreat with you. Scholarship their registration fee so there are fewer obstacles to their attendance. Host a Bible study on the life of Jesus, with a few friends who are interested in learning Christ's claims. Invite a neighbor to a prayer breakfast to hear the story of how a respected leader came to the Lord. Most of all, prayerfully ask individuals who trust you, if they would like to trust Jesus.

"They said to the woman, 'We no longer believe just because of what you said; now we have heard for ourselves, and we know that this man really is the Savior of the world'" (John 4:42).

Prayer
Heavenly Father, give me the courage, love, and grace to boldly speak salvation through faith in Jesus.

Application

Who do I know that I can share the good news of Jesus Christ with?

Originally published July 24, 2019, at WisdomHunters.com

ABOUT THE 3:15 PROJECT

The 3:15 Project helps Christians know and share their story. Based in Atlanta, Georgia, 315 advocates for, connects, equips, and empowers ministry and church leaders locally and around the world to launch and develop fruitful story ministries.

Visit 315project.com for more information.

ABOUT STEPS OF COURAGE

Steps of Courage is a guided journey designed to help people walk deeper with God, and come ever closer to knowing and sharing their story wholeheartedly.

Visit StepsOfCourage.com for more information.

ABOUT STORYDRIVE

StoryDrive is a cooperative that helps drive growth and transformation in people and organizations through the power of personal stories. This is accomplished through research, investing, consulting, coaching, teaching, and creating fruitful partnerships.

Visit storydrive.com for more information.

Listen to the Stories of Hope Podcast

search for "315 Project stories of hope"
in your favorite podcast player
or point your phone camera at the images below:

apple   **spotify**

Free eBook:
Standing Up a Story Ministry

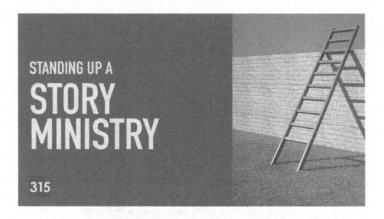

What's a "story ministry" and how can it help a
church realize growth and transformation?
This eBook helps cast a vision and spark
conversations among leaders.

Visit 315project.com/ebooks or
point your phone's camera at this image: